Are you for real?

Are you for real?

MENTAL HEALTH IN THE MISINFORMATION AGE

Dr. Douglas E Tomson

ISBN-13: 9781977911629
ISBN-10: 1977911625

Table of Contents

Introduction

I n spite of the fact that we can expect to be healthier, live longer, and have more wealth than any previous generation we find ourselves facing epidemic levels of anxiety, depression, and loneliness; as well as, soaring rates of consuming, using, and abusing whatever we can get our hands on.

As a Vietnam Veteran who returned home with PTSD, I understand things like struggling to establish and maintain close relationships, repressed anger, and feeling numb and emotionally detached from other people. As a licensed clinical psychologist, I have learned about healing and personal growth.

In a technology driven rapidly changing world, where suicide is now the number one cause of death *internationally*, it takes a warrior's spirit and courage to resist the temptation to be dishonest, *in*-authentic, and *self*-alienated. That "safe" emotional distance we use to protect ourselves leaves us disconnected and *self*-alienated.

The truth is there is no "silver bullet" for mental health. We can't fix people, heal people, or protect people from themselves. Mental health is an inside job. This book is part memoir, part manifesto of mental health. It acknowledges that when we fail to give our brain direction, it will run on and on, repeating old thinking patterns until we get bored, sick, or until someone else finds a way to run it for us.

This book will teach you how to gain control of your thinking and develop genuine relationships based on honesty, empathy, and intimacy by learning to ask yourself **Five (5) Critical Questions.**

It will teach you the skills you need to step-up and find the courage and warrior-spirit you need to take control of your life. The process is simple, proven, and so empowering you'll wonder how you didn't discover it yourself.

I encourage you to keep reading.

CHAPTER 1

What I Learned in Prison

California's prison system was once considered to be the model of progressive penology nationwide. By the 1980s however, the system was bulging at the seams. The system eventually reached 155 percent of its design capacity. Inmates were housed two to a cell and prisoners were confined to their cells almost all of the time. The entire system became a violent, dangerous place for both inmates and guards. The violence was rampant; the rats roamed at will and the plumbing leaked so badly that correctional officials considered issuing chamber pots to the inmates. The incidents of armed assaults among prisoners rose from two hundred per year to more than eight hundred a year.

Deuel Vocational Institution (DVI) is one of the thirty-three prisons in the California penal system. After DVI had double-celled all of its inmates, it started housing new prisoners in the day rooms. As more and more prisoners kept coming, the prison began housing inmates in the gymnasium, and when that filled up, it housed prisoners in the old laundry room.

DVI was not only dangerously overcrowded, but it also had a history of violence. When you stand inside the fence at DVI, you're standing in the spot where the notorious Mexican Mafia gang first spilled blood in 1957. It was famous for the fights and homicides that took place inside its walls. DVI was referred to by both inmates and staff as the "Gladiator School," and in 1987 DVI was labeled "the stabbing capital of the world."

Men locked up for long periods of time can become ingenious at making weapons out of almost anything. They can make a crude form of gunpowder out of ground-up match heads. A newspaper can be turned into a deadly spear by rolling it into a long tube and fitting the end with a piece of sharp metal. When you walk the tiers and gauntlets inside the yards and corridors at DVI you can get bumped, hit, kicked, and even stabbed with a flying dart. Add in a little fear and rage and it's not difficult to imagine how things can get out of hand very quickly.

So, what kind of fool would voluntarily enter a place like DVI?

I entered DVI as a staff psychologist in 2007. Before that, I spent a decade facilitating year-long *anger management* and *domestic violence* groups for the Riverside County Probation Department. My experiences in those programs taught me that if you want to change someone's behavior, you need to change the way he or she thinks. I wanted to see if I could apply that insight to rehabilitate and motivate men already in prison to change and grow.

After being put under federal receivership, every new inmate at DVI had to be screened for possible mental illnesses and inclusion into the prison's mental health-care system. I was one of the psychologists selected to make that determination. At that time, the prevailing logic of the correctional system was, "Do the crime, do the time." The primary focus was to control the bad guys by locking them up. It was known as the "waste management" model of corrections.

I started my tenure at DVI working in the reception center, screening new inmates for possible mental illnesses. The first thing I learned was that there weren't many "new" inmates. I rarely encountered an inmate who was in prison for the first time. It wasn't uncommon to hear an inmate reply, "I don't remember," when I asked how many times he had been in prison. It was often the case that he had been incarcerated ten or more times.

I learned very quickly that prison isn't a deterrent for these men. In fact, most of them treated their incarceration as an opportunity to reconnect with old friends. It was a chance to share stories, catch up on family news, and reminisce about the good old days. It also provides them with the opportunity to get treatment for long- neglected medical, dental, and psychological problems. The most important thing I learned, however, was that they knew a lot more about the system and how it works than I did.

Since mental health symptoms are *subjective* experiences, it was a constant struggle for me to determine if the symptoms they were reporting to me were genuine. Then, one day I confiscated a letter from an inmate I was interviewing. It spelled out precisely what he needed to know to convince someone he had a "mental illness." It's a little hard to read through all of the details, but it is a wealth of information should you ever find yourself in the unfortunate predicament of being locked up in a place like DVI.

<u>How to Malinger</u>
LETTER FROM ONE INMATE TO ANOTHER

Now concerning SSI. you want lifetime SSI, then you got to go with the Mental Health. First, you got to build up a history. This is how to do it. First you got to go to psych doctor and tell him that you are always paranoid and feeling like your scared. Don't play it like your "too" crazy, but play it like your edgy, uneasy. Tell him you would like some medication because you can't sleep, and when you do it is only for a couple of hours, waking up sweating, etc., scared. Your scared to attend yard because people are after you. Tell them you use to get that way when you were young. Pick a state other than California and tell them from age 10-14 you took psychiatric care. Make up a doctor's name. Believe me they don't check another state. Then tell them you started using cocaine and your fear attacks started getting worse. You thought it was only the cocaine. Then you quit cocaine for over three years, but you still can't shake the attacks. You feel the police is trying to get you killed. Some times your okay for a while, but then sometimes you get to the point where you can't keep it under control. Now remember no crazy person feels they are crazy, so you can't go in there telling them you're a nut because they will see through it. What you get to do is tell them the symptoms you are feeling, (fear, paranoia, hearing voices, hearing the people around you plotting, etc.) Now what to do is get medication. Once you get that, you bring such paper work to the mental health, or use it for when you apply for SSI (in here) before you leave. You can apply for SSI in here through the mental health Social Worker. First you have to be getting treatment, have pills prescribed, etc. See the psych regularly, say the medication is not working so you can get a higher dosage. Your never gonna take the pills. Put it under your tongue and spit it out. Give the doctor a spacey look, and always fumble your hands, or fidget around. Look over your shoulder etc. Tell them you also took medication when you were young. Tell them it was called Trillion and Cogentin. Trillion is an antipsychotic medication, Cogentin is a medication that doesn't allow you to have seizures or side effects. Tell him you were on it from 10-14, 32 mg of Trilifon and 15 mg of Cogent. When you sound like you know what you are talking about they give you that. If you don't know something just say you don't know or remember. This is a quick rub down, what you don't understand ask me___ you've got the whole concept. Here's what you want to change your medication. The reason why it looks better for your case history. Because I show extensive case history. Like Thorazine wouldn't work so they tried a knew twist. Now what you want to start doing is getting copies of all your case history in your cell because when you do apply you don't have to try and get copies. It cuts the time process down. Also county jail mental health records can also be used. The more the better. Just start getting those records. Now don't tell the psych people you want records yet. First get on the "new" meds. Don't let them feel you want a specific brand, just say your other doctors was gonna switch you from Trilifon and Cogentin. A lot of time Thorazine is used for behavior problems. Now keep this, once you get out you can go to the Department of Rehabilitation and show you are getting SSI. They will lend you money for clothes. Also they will help you get in some college or trade school. More money. But your plan is good. But get your history file. Get a couple of stamped envelopes and write the county jail asking for your mental health county files. Then send them a pre-stamped envelope with your name and address on it. Or if you want, wait until you get your medication. Then after a short while, get the mental health worker to help you get your file from county. Then ask her to get SSI form. She might say she doesn't know how but that's drama. Apply close to go days before release. You will need payee. All else you need to know, ask.

The Hole

After three years in the reception center, I was reassigned to the administrative segregation unit. The "ad seg" unit, the "hotbox," "the hole," and "SHU" are all references to solitary confinement. Solitary confinement is a special form of incarceration where a prisoner is isolated away from the rest of the prison population. When a prisoner is considered dangerous to himself or others, is suspected of organizing or being engaged in illegal or gang activities, or is at a high risk of being harmed by other inmates, he is sent to "the hole." It's also a form of protective custody for pedophiles, witnesses, and inmates with a different sexual orientation.

For the next three years, I worked with a population of prisoners who experienced anger with such frequency and intensity that everyone who dealt with them had to armor up. That means wearing a protective vest, goggles, and having a custody officer with me at all times. These men would get angry whenever they failed to get their way. If they got bored, they would stir up the excitement they needed to feel alive while being incarcerated. Whenever I conducted groups, I had to sit in the middle of a circle of wire cages, which I referred to as "therapeutic modules."

The most common complaint I heard from these men was "racing thoughts." This rapid cycling of their thoughts helped them avoid their feelings and ignore their surroundings. However, as their appetite for excitement grew, it would lead to a vicious cycle. Because they felt less and less, confinement affected them less and less.

After working with repeat offenders for over three years in *both* the reception center and administrative segregation, I happened to meet the Catholic chaplain at lunch one day. We had a long conversation about our experiences and personal reasons for choosing to come and work in prison. The chaplain's goal was to get these men interested in attending his services. I was interested in doing something more along the lines of rehabilitation than "waste management." He wanted to attract more interest in his sermons, and he asked me if I would be interested in helping him do that.

Following our conversation, we decided to see if we could work together to inspire some of these men to change. At the chaplain's request, I began doing short talks before his services in an effort to share with them what the research had to say about them and what I had personally experienced and learned from working with them. I confronted them *directly* about things like accountability, individual responsibility and changing the way they think. I challenged them to evolve into the men their children and families needed them to be and the men they were *meant* to be. In the beginning, only eight or ten inmates showed up for these little talks. As these men told other men what they were learning about themselves, the numbers began to mount. Within a month, the chaplain counted over one hundred men in attendance.

These talks proved to be more productive than we had hoped. The Chaplain said each talk increased the number of inmates who attended his next service. To give you a sense of what these talks were like, this is a transcript of the talk I gave at DVI on March 31, 2011.

Good morning, and thank you for that warm reception. I want to take a moment and try and bring everyone up to speed.

I'm Dr. Tomson and I'm a clinical psychologist here at DVI.

I'm here today to talk to you about people... you, me, everyone.

In addition to being a psychologist here at DVI, I'm also a Vietnam vet. Because of that, many people consider me to be a warrior. I believe I'm a warrior, but not because I served in Vietnam. I believe I'm a warrior because of the way I choose to live my life.

One of the things I believe in is telling the truth. One thing I know to be true is there are more jails and prisons in the United States than colleges and universities. What I want to talk about today is why you're here, and not in one of those colleges or universities.

Another thing I know to be true is those of us who work in the correctional health- care system cannot change you, or fix you. No one can do that but you. However, I'm hoping that what you hear in here today might change the way you think, because what got you here is the way you think.

I was thinking about what I wanted to say to you this morning about what it means to be "responsible." In simple terms, being

responsible means doing the things you need to do, to keep from being sent to places like DVI.

The truth is, I've struggled with some of the same issues many of you have. My struggle has been with my anger. I can go from zero to sixty in a heartbeat, and I turn into the Lone Ranger, constantly on the lookout for some wrong to make right. My reward for growing up is this: I'm free to do the things I want to do and live the way I choose to live.

I have come to believe that what you need to do, is learn how to develop better interpersonal and communication skills. You need these skills to help you develop the healthy relationships you need to grow and stay out of prison.

There are certain "criminal thinking patterns" that tend to get people into places like this. I'd like to review a couple of those "criminal thinking patterns" with you this morning.

The first one is called "mollification." Mollification sounds like this: "If I hadn't been raised in hell, I would never have gotten into crime"; or "I would never have gotten into crime if I hadn't gotten addicted to drugs"; or "If I had loving parents I wouldn't have resorted to crime."

We cannot be objective about ourselves. We only learn the truth about ourselves through honest interaction with other people. If I don't have someone who will tell me the truth, then my view of myself will be distorted by my limited perspective. This applies to you, me, and everyone else you will ever meet.

The bottom line is this: you're no different from the rest of us; you're accountable for the things you do.

Another problematic thinking pattern is called "compartmentalization." You compartmentalize when you split off pieces of your personality to avoid taking responsibility for yourself. What that means is, you behave differently depending on who you're with and where you are. If you continue to behave this way you will never develop a real sense of who you are.

This splitting off of your personality will separate you from your feelings, and this is a terrible price to pay because you need your feelings to make good decisions. Your mind will come up with options but you need your feelings to select the best option. Once you start making bad decisions, you can find yourself in a place like this overnight.

People who compartmentalize their lives can be fearless and fearful at the same time. They can be grandiose and meek at the same time. This is because they have separated themselves from their real feelings and they don't know who they are or what they believe. Their value system is not "integrated."

Let's say I'm driving my favorite shortcut to work one day, and I hit a big pothole that wasn't there the day before. The next day I drive to work and I hit that same pothole again because I forgot there was a pothole that wasn't there two days ago. On the third day, on my way to work, I hit that damn pothole again because it's a habit for me to drive that shortcut to work.

On the fourth day, I remember that pothole, so I drive around it, but I haven't learned anything or changed. I only change on the fifth day when I drive to work on a new route. It took me five days to adapt and grow.

By the way, continuing to hit that pothole is a metaphor for prison and parole. If you fail to learn from your mistakes and change, you will continue to recycle back into prison, and your whole life will pass before you know it. Know this: if you're sitting in this room with me today, there's a seventy-eight percent chance you will continue to commit crimes and come back here again. There's a seventy-eight percent chance that you won't change.

Habitual lying is another way to separate yourself from your feelings, and the result will be anger and confusion. Other people will not understand you, and as a consequence, you will feel chronically angry and misunderstood. That's because this way of avoiding responsibility is a vicious cycle.

Remember, we can't fix you. Nobody can do that but you. All we can do is medicate you, which may help you get through the day, but it will also prevent you from feeling and thereby growing.

Your challenge is to start reeling in those bits and pieces of yourself. That means learning to behave with integrity, regardless of the circumstances. A person with integrity behaves the same way regardless of who is around. They do the right thing because it's the right thing to do. I know what you're thinking: "How boring!"

When you compartmentalize your life, you feel less and less. When this happens, your life will shrink down to fear, excitement, and boredom. Those are the only feelings you will be able to experience. And if life gets too boring you will stir things up to get the excitement, and stimulation you need. This is survival mode, and it means you have become addicted to excitement.

If you should decide you want to change, you have to make a fundamental shift in your thinking, in your attitude about life, and in your relationships with other people.

True happiness in life requires doing something meaningful with your life. The fundamental change I'm talking about is finding something in your life you can commit to, something that is bigger and more important than your needs. I know that's a difficult concept for you to grasp, but it's critical that you do.

That's what I'm doing here today. I'm trying to do something meaningful, trying to a make a difference. Start today to experience your feelings, all of them. And, stop lying and compartmentalizing your life to avoid being accountable. If you can learn that lesson now, not twenty years from now, you won't have to waste your life in prison.

Be clear about this: in spite of how smart you think you are, the system is big enough and motivated enough that it will eventually catch you if you continue to commit crimes. No one wins all the time. And know this: once you're in the system its hell to get out.

And by the way, the system is broken. We know incarcerating you won't change you. For one thing, you don't learn from your mistakes. We can't beat "criminal thinking patterns" out of you either, we've tried that too. No one can change you but you. If we could change you, we would have done that a long time ago and then we could all go home.

Last week I told a story about an experience I had while driving home one night from working out. I was at a traffic light and there were two lanes of cars waiting. There was a car in front of me and one next to me, and we were all waiting for the light to turn green.

Out of the corner of my eye I saw a kid on a bicycle heading for the intersection from a side street. I watched him decide to speed up and try and get across that intersection before that light changed.

As the light turned to green, he raced across the intersection in front of those two cars. The first car just missed him and the second car slowed down enough to avoid hitting him.

I watched that kid throw all caution to the wind for a split second of excitement. Once he got safely across the street, he threw his arms up to the sky and "flipped off" the two cars. The excitement lasted only a second or two, but it was enough to reinforce his recklessness.

I notice some of you are laughing because you realize that kid is you!

I promise you that kid is headed to DVI, sooner or later. That's because he will likely do something like that one too many times. And like I said, no one wins all the time.

I also admitted last week I wanted to knock that kid off that bicycle. I thought he needed a good lesson in life. Fortunately, I wasn't in a position to act on that impulse, but I was tempted. The system is poised and ready for that youngster because it only takes a second or two to make a bad decision. I fought for your right to live your life the way you want to, but I want to caution you about what meaning you attach to that statement.

It does not mean you can do whatever you want when other people are involved. When you make short-term decisions based on your need for excitement, you will make bad decisions.

An inmate once said to me, "Hey Doc, come on, just fix me!" I realized he not only thought I could fix him, but he thought I was holding out on him. Know this: if I could fix you, we wouldn't be sitting here together right now.

So, my question to you this morning is this: "Do you want to spend the rest of your life as a petulant teenager, or are you ready to grow up and make peace with the rest of us?" You have an opportunity to grow and turn your life around.

It's in your hands.

Thank you for coming today.

Lifers

While I was doing talks for the chaplain, I heard about a "lifer" at DVI who had a reputation for being not only a model prisoner but an accomplished artisan. A "lifer" is a reference to someone who has an "indeterminate" life sentence, as in, "seven years to life," or "twenty-five years to life." The dictionary defines *limbo* as "a place or state of oblivion" and anyone serving an *in*-determinate life sentence knows what it's like to live in a state of oblivion.

When I got the opportunity to see some of the vases and ceramics this man was creating, I decided I needed to meet him. I had never seen anything like the incredible pieces of art this man was crafting. Each piece was unique and perfectly formed as if it had come out of a mold. They featured swirls of brilliant colors, many of them were over two feet tall, and they were all trimmed in gold. I learned that one of his pieces sold for $1,900 on the Internet. The contrast between those vases and those dull, drab prison walls was extraordinary.

So, one day I walked into the prison hobby shop and asked about where I could find this man, even though I didn't know his name or his CDC number. Within minutes I was introduced to "KK." The first thing I noticed was a middle-aged man quietly working alone in the cramped corner of a tiny room. He was covered from head to toe in fine white dust. Beneath the dust, I could see he was immaculately groomed. His hair was combed, he was clean-shaven, and his clothes were perfectly pressed.

I introduced myself and told him I was interested in talking to him about the beautiful ceramics he was creating, as well as the life he had created for himself while living in oblivion. I wanted to understand what he had done to survive, even thrive, from deep inside a culture of conflict, despair, and violence.

KK told me he completed every vocational program the system had in the first ten years of his incarceration.

After all of these programs were abandoned due to poor funding and overcrowding, he started spending his time in the prison hobby shop, which was the only venue still available to him. For the next fifteen years, he taught himself how to throw clay on a tiny potter's wheel and fire the clay in a small kiln. In the process, he taught himself how to mix paint, and he even developed his own unique glazes through trial and error.

In the beginning, there were no supplies or other resources, so he wrote to suppliers he found in trade magazines asking them questions and requesting samples of their products. I was so captivated by him and his story that I began dropping in on him whenever I had some free time so we could talk.

No matter when I arrived, he would immediately stop whatever he was doing, find a stool often covered in dust, wipe off the dust, and politely invite me to sit so we could talk. I was always treated as an honored guest in his home. Our discussions had a powerful uplifting effect on me. I would leave eager to return so we could pick up where we had left off.

In the beginning, our discussions centered on things like coping with life in prison, avoiding conflict, dealing with difficult people, and issues related to securing parole. Over time our conversations turned philosophical as we talked about how some people can maintain their sanity under seemingly hopeless conditions.

In response to one of our conversations I gave him a copy of Viktor Frankl's book, *Man's Search for Meaning*. This book led to some fascinating exchanges and insights related to being incarcerated in prison, in contrast to the *virtual* prisons so many people build for themselves out of fear and self-imposed limitations.

KK shared with me that every Friday night he and a small group of other lifers got together in that tiny room and talked about the same kinds of things he and I were discussing. KK had spent much of his time studying the intrica-cies of dealing with *both* the court system and the parole board, and he would share his knowledge with these other men.

Eventually, KK invited me to sit in on one of these weekly meetings. I was able to see and hear for myself the kind of things they talked about and what they were doing to atone for their life crimes. On the very first night, I accepted their invitation to start working together to see if I could help them develop the insights and skills the parole board wanted to see from them before they granted them parole.

Currently, a lifer stands about an eight-teen percent chance of being granted parole by the parole board. In the past, the rate has been close to zero. The occasions of a lifer convicted of murder getting parole, and not having the decision reversed by the governor have been rare.

In late 2011, the parole board determined KK was suitable for parole and he was given a release date after more than twenty-five years of confinement. What followed were many months of waiting for the governor's response, postponements, and delays. True to his character, KK never wavered or failed to maintain a sense of dignity and class while dealing with these disappoint-ments. Then one day, he was notified to get ready, and the very next day he was released. His release brought an end of one of the most meaningful rela-tionships I had ever forged.

CHAPTER 2

The Most Dangerous Man Alive

My relationship with KK was so empowering, I decided to do my best to carry on what he started in the back of that tiny room in the prison hobby shop. I established some clear goals and objectives, and this informal gathering of lifers became an official *education*-based rehabilitation program at Deuel Vocational Institute called the *"INSIGHT Program."*

The INSIGHT Program was open to any inmate at DVI who was serving an *in*-determinate life sentence and had the possibility of paroling one day. The stated purpose of the *INSIGHT Program* was to teach these men the character and communication skills they needed to discuss the very personal issues the parole board wanted them to discuss. Also, I wanted to teach them how to behave according to the values, beliefs, and principles of responsible people, not just become someone who doesn't commit crimes. I took on the role of teacher, mentor and in some cases the parent they never had.

Over a period of three years, thirty-eight different lifers participated in *The INSIGHT Program*. Most of these men had committed their life crimes when they were in their twenties and hadn't committed another serious crime in over twenty years. Many of them had managed to maintain contact with their families, but a few had become like a stray dog that nobody wanted. Most of them started out thinking they could whip the system, but twenty or thirty years later the system was all they knew.

Most of them had dropped out of school at an early age so their thinking was very concrete. When you perceive life as a series of independent events, it's hard to learn from your mistakes. What these men lacked were fundamental concepts of work, education, and interpersonal relationships. In essence, what they needed more than anything else was to be "reparented."

The INSIGHT Program was unique in the correctional system because we were allowed to meet without any custody staff present. It was just myself and as many as seventeen lifers locked up together in a big room. This allowed for honesty and genuine interpersonal interaction, which was a new experience for most of these men. The groups met every Thursday afternoon for two hours. I recorded and reviewed every session so I could determine what I thought worked and what didn't work. Very few people today understand what a superior experience living *authentically* can be. I can say in the end, I left every session a better man than when I went in.

The Prison Code

Anyone who has ever seen a show about prison, worked in prison, or been in prison knows about the "prison code." It's a reference to a phenomenon known as "hypermasculinity" that prevails in the prison culture. It involves assuming a tough, nonfeeling exterior as a way of protecting yourself against violence and exploitation.

The prison code requires that you mind your own business, suffer in silence, and never admit to being afraid. You must appear to be tough and never help authorities in any way. You trust no one and must always be ready to fight, or at least look as though you're willing to fight. Just accepting the challenge to fight is enough to earn the respect of other inmates, regardless of the outcome. Refusing to fight, however, is considered the ultimate act of cowardice. If you don't pick up on the rules you become an example. When questioned by authorities, you didn't see anything, you didn't hear anything, and you don't know anything.

In addition to struggling to overcome the prison code, I had to deal with the fact that no one tells the truth in prison. That's because telling the truth can get you into a lot of trouble. Being labeled a "snitch" or a "rat" can get you killed. In time, I learned that trying to get the men in the group to tell the truth was not only a bad idea, it was a dangerous idea.

A Warrior Culture

My own experience in dealing with a "warrior culture" gave me some insight into dealing with the prison code. In 1966, I was a naive young kid playing basketball on scholarship for the University of California, Santa Barbara. That year, we played UCLA's freshman basketball team which included Lew Alcindor (now Kareem Abdul-Jabbar). That freshman team had just beaten the *two-time* National Champion *varsity* team 75-60. They went 21- 0 and outscored their opponents by an average of fifty-seven points a game!

In addition to that little brush with reality, I remember spending a lot of time in the gym, struggling to find and make it to my classes on time (UCSB is spread out over acres of land along the California coastline) and thinking I wanted to go to medical school someday. I was living in the *San Miguel* dorm with a number of other athletes, traveling everywhere by bicycle, hanging out in Isla Vista and eating in the cafeteria three times a day. *Batman* was the number-one show on television and I also remember watching nightly news reports about the war in Vietnam. Two years later, I was a "surgical assistant" working in the operating room of the 27th MASH hospital in Chu Lai, Vietnam.

For reasons only a nineteen-year-old kid could possibly compehend, in the summer following my freshman year, I made a foolish and fateful decision. I dropped out of school, joined the army and volunteered to serve in Vietnam as a "surgical assistant." Did I mention I was young and *very* naive? The next thing I remember, was some drill sergeant screaming at me while I was having my head shaved in boot camp at Fort Polk, Louisiana.

Boot camp breaks you down and then builds you back up with a new set of beliefs and values. The process indoctrinates you into a "warrior culture" that de-emphasizes emotion and individuality and focuses instead on group bonding. It also establishes a sense of strong brotherhood and self-sacrifice. The process creates men who will fight and kill for their country. In some cases, the effects of the process can stay with men for the rest of their lives. I believe it took two decades of PTSD, many failed relationships, and finally a doctorate in psychology to identify and change the effects it had on me.

During my advanced training to be a surgical assistant, I was told that I wasn't being trained to go to war. No sir, I was an important part of the new

Pacification Program that was going to bring peace to South Vietnam. I was going to make a difference.

No amount of training can prepare you for the kind of suffering that occurs in war. I arrived in Chu Lai at the height of the war, during the Tet Offensive in 1968. Within the first seven days, I was formally introduced to the *Pacification Program* in an emergency room full of men covered in blood, grime, and dirt. These men had been injured on the battlefield only fifteen minutes earlier. The emergency room was filled wall-to-wall with casualties.

Many of them were missing parts of their bodies, a foot, or an arm or a leg, and others had abdominal and chest wounds. People everywhere were starting IVs and doing what they could to help. What I remember most was the smell of burnt flesh and men screaming in the kind of pain that even morphine couldn't stop. Suddenly, someone yelled at me, "Do what you can for that guy"!

A soldier was lying motionless on a stretcher on his back, and he didn't appear to have a scratch on him, *except* for a large piece of metal sticking straight out of the front of his head. It had pierced his metal helmet from above and entered directly into his cranium about two inches, just above his hairline. When I got to the stretcher, he spoke to me! He said, "You guys are the greatest." It had only been a few minutes, and he was grateful for how quickly he had been evacuated to a hospital and help. I started an IV, monitored his vital signs, noticed the bleeding had stopped, and noted that he was stable.

That's when I learned about *triage.* When there are multiple casualties, someone has to decide the priority of who gets treatment first and who has to wait. Those decisions determine who has the greatest chance of survival and who must wait because their injuries are more severe and potentially fatal. The *triage* officer determined that the soldier with the head injury was going to have to wait. It was far too risky to try and do anything. He needed to be evacuated to Japan where there was a neurosurgeon.

Since he was stable, there wasn't much more anyone could do for him. So, I spent the next six hours keeping him stable and calm by holding his hand and talking to him as he lapsed into and out of consciousness. During that long wait he never once asked me what was wrong, or what his injuries were. He kept thanking me for all we were doing to help him and the other men. I have never felt more helpless or powerless than I did sitting there holding that soldier's hand. I still have flashbacks of that experience and often wonder what happened to that brave soldier.

While I was in Vietnam, my commander in chief threw in the towel and *both* Dr. Martin Luther King and Robert Kennedy were assassinated. The day I learned that Robert Kennedy had been killed, I was sitting on my bunk in an old army tent, in the sweltering heat, somewhere in Southeast Asia. I remember thinking the whole world must be at war, and I wasn't going to survive this nightmare. I thought my life was going to be over before it started, and no one would even notice, or care and for what?

For fifteen months, I struggled to maintain my sanity, but I never spoke about the things I was witnessing or the things I was feeling. Like everyone else, I put my feelings aside so I could do what I had to do. I tried to get through the whole experience without feelings. This proved to be both a blessing and a curse.

When I returned home, I was emotionally numb. I had a difficult time relating to anyone, including my own family. It felt to me like I was living in an entirely different world than the one I left behind just a year before. What happened to the "Summer of Love"? Within a month of my return home, Neil Armstrong was walking on the moon, and one month after that, Woodstock happened. I was lost and confused.

Vietnam was a conflict within a conflict, and there was even conflict about the conflict. Instead of a "Welcome Home," people were shouting things like "Warmonger" and "Baby killer." So, I did my best to keep my mouth shut, blend in, and forget the whole experience. I just wanted to move on with my life.

I went back to school at UCSB. I even went to the Haight /Ashbury district in San Francisco looking for the "hippies" I had heard about when I was in Vietnam, but they were already gone. Things seemed to go well for a while, but I experienced what I now know was "survivor's guilt" and an uncomfortable sense that something wasn't right. The Pacification Program looked a lot like war to me. I felt betrayed, and I was bitter and angry.

I made it into my third year of medical school before my midlife crisis hit. After all of the struggle and sacrifice, I went through to get into medical school I experienced flashbacks, and I had a change of heart. I began to question my decision to become a doctor. Somewhere along the line, I decided to be a doctor and I got lost in the struggle. I was handling all the coursework, the stress and the long hours well, but I realized I had no idea what I wanted to do.

I recalled that on my first day of medical school one of the professors stood up and said, "There's never been a doctor, from Hippocrates on, who ever cured or healed anyone of anything. The human body does that. We treat pain and suffering." That memory and the thought of a lifetime filled with more pain and suffering became overwhelming. So, I made another fateful decision. This time I dropped out of medical school.

That decision proved to be the last straw for my family. I wasn't able to find the words to adequately explain my decision and they weren't too eager to try to understand my decision anyway. It didn't take long for them to lose interest in me and my struggles. They disconnected emotionally, and I found myself doing the same. Unfortunately, we became estranged, and I was never able to regain their trust or support again.

In the free fall that ensued, I took a job as a bouncer/bartender in the biggest nightclub in the San Fernando Valley of Los Angeles. I went from my son the doctor to my son the bouncer quicker than you could say, "What the fuck did he do this time?"

The nightclub was called Big Daddy's, and it was the hot spot in town. It was three stories tall, and each floor had a huge dance floor with two or three long bars. Each bar had three bartenders and a team of bouncers. There was a disco with a big *disco-ball* on the top floor; rock 'n' roll playing on the middle floor, and a country and western bar with country music playing on the bottom floor.

Working at Big Daddy's was like living in a movie, or being in one of those *Xbox* or *PlayStation* games with non-stop action. It wasn't unusual to have as many as a thousand people come into the club on any given Saturday night. Every night something memorable happened. One night, I remember being lifted up by my hair and thrown down a flight of stairs. As I was tumbling head over heels down those stairs, I remember thinking to myself; "You better land on your feet fool, because that other fool is right behind you!"

I viewed the whole experience as a way for me to make some money behind the bar and, at the same time, work out my anger *righteously*. To me, that meant beating the shit out of "bullies," meaning anyone looking for a fight. I thought I could use the adrenaline high to do something constructive with my anger. It was wild and crazy and exciting.

However, I experienced certain unsettling things that brought me to my senses. I realized my anger wasn't going away and I was just using the job as a way to justify my anger. My plan for working out my anger by beating the shit out of people wasn't *really* working out.

So, with very little planning and no clear destination in mind, I quit that job, took the money I had saved, and set out in search of myself. During my trek, I visited the Prado museum and sampled home-made *paella* at a family campground on the outskirts of Madrid. On a beautiful Sunday afternoon, I watched a bullfight in Granada, high in the mountains of Spain. I took a ferry across the Strait of Gibraltar to Northern Africa, where I experienced the Tangiers market place, ate lunch at a local café and walked to the famous *Kasbah*. I arrived in Hong Kong just in time for the Chinese New Year and while there, watched little kids eat candied chicken feet like they were a delicacy. I made it as far as Australia where I toured the Sydney Opera House and spent three months living on North Bondi Beach.

Here's what I learned. When there's no one around to rely on but yourself, you learn how to take care of yourself. I know that sounds corny and trite, but the more you figure things out for yourself, the quicker you realize how much potential you have. One of the best lessons I learned was this: if I make a poor decision, I can change it, and make a better one.

That time alone gave me the freedom I needed to focus on what I really wanted to do with my life. Likely because of my personal struggles, I wanted to define what it means to be "mentally healthy." With that as my goal, I went back to school. This time my plan was to study psychology. For the next decade, I worked two, and sometimes three, jobs at a time to pay for school.

While attending graduate school, I waited tables; managed apartments; taught courses in general psychology, abnormal psychology, and human sexuality; worked with other Vietnam veterans; facilitated groups; and counseled both individuals and couples. After spending time in three separate graduate programs, I eventually completed a doctorate in clinical psychology and became a licensed clinical psychologist.

The knowledge I gained while completing the doctorate changed me, and I discovered what an important role our emotions play in our lives. Learning how to honor and express *my* feelings gave me insight into the price I was paying for trying to *think* my way through life (a trick I learned in Vietnam). I used that insight to help the men in the *INSIGHT Program* reconnect with their feelings. Unfortunately, getting these men to feel again wasn't enough to automatically change their behavior. To truly change, I had to replace their criminal thinking patterns with new ways of thinking.

Understanding and Insight

In 2009, the California Supreme Court ruled that an inmate's "lack of understanding" together with a "denial of responsibility" continued to make an inmate a risk to public safety. The California Board of Parole had similarly cited a "lack of insight" as the number one reason for denying a prisoner parole. The parole board also made it clear they didn't want to hear an inmate say he had "accepted full responsibility" for his life crime. They wanted to hear the inmate talk *precisely* about what he has accepted responsibility for.

One of my biggest challenges was convincing these men their struggle wasn't with the "Board," or the board members, or with drugs or alcohol, but with themselves. When we don't know how we feel and we don't have healthy ways to deal with our feelings, we're vulnerable to whatever it is that will help us keep those feelings contained. We use things like alcohol and drugs, excitement, sex, gambling and even too much thinking to avoid dealing with our emotions. Over time we become dependent on these behaviors to rescue us from ourselves. These men needed to learn how to get out of their heads and the into their hearts. To do that, they had to develop the communication skills they needed to talk about their feelings, including any remorse they had for their life crime.

In the beginning, the group and I spent many hours rationally discussing the issues and questions the board members wanted them to be able to discuss. However, it didn't appear to me that they were learning the things I thought they should be learning.

Since both "understanding" and "insight" are inherently unscientific and unquantifiable criteria, the courts and the people on the board are forced to rely on their *subjective* impressions rather than facts when making their decisions. Talking about feelings in the abstract removes us from the actual feeling state. So, I began creating situations where I could confront their feelings *directly*, particularly, their anger, by getting them angry at me, if necessary. That allowed me the opportunity to teach them how to defuse their anger in real time.

The Hot Seat

The group functioned like a basketball team with me as the head coach. If they wanted to get into the game (get on the "Hot Seat"), they had to be willing to talk in the *first* person about their crimes and answer the very personal questions the board wanted them to talk about. Here are some of the parole board questions:

> **Did you intend to kill your victim?**
> **What was your specific role in the crime? Were you the leader, or were you more of a follower or an accomplice?**
> **What were your character defects at the time of the crime as opposed to the type of character have you built for yourself now?**
> **What coping skills have you learned and utilized since the crime occurred?**

Because participation in the *INSIGHT Program* was entirely voluntary, I had no qualms about confronting these men man-to-man and face-to-face. There were many times when you could cut the tension in the room with a feather. If they sat on the bench and wouldn't voluntarily get on the Hot Seat and talk to me, I removed them from the program because there was a waiting list of men who wanted to join. The men in the group started referring to me as "The Most Dangerous Man Alive" because I made them feel, and then I made them talk about their feelings.

I wanted these men to learn how to control their anger and violent tendencies in the moment. So, I was always looking for the slightest suggestion of arrogance or attitude to confront. I used to say to them, "You don't have to sit there and take this shit from me. You can walk out of here right now." No one ever did. To be honest, this approach didn't always work. Some men stopped coming, and I drove away those who I thought weren't serious.

Self-disclosure is the process of first, being aware of your thoughts, feelings, and beliefs; and second, expressing these truths honestly to another person. "Self-disclosure" switches to "self-presentation" the moment someone tries to use what they say to get a particular response from the person he or she is speaking to.

My job was trying to distinguish one from the other.

The INSIGHT Model of Communication

The INSIGHT Model of Communication was developed to overcome the prison code and the resistance these men had to talking about the truth. To use the model, you have to understand that there is no one reality; there is no one truth about anything. We each use our five senses to create perceptions about the world, which we then use to construct our particular view of reality.

Although it's true that we each construct our unique view of reality, we each do so with precisely the same mechanism, the human nervous system. Since everyone's nervous system operates in precisely the same way, this model was created to represent and account for the three (3) different levels of human experience: *objective* (facts), *subjective* (thoughts and feelings) and *inter-subjective* (meanings). Together, these three types of experiences combine to form our perceptions of reality. Each of us is unique in the way he or she combines these experiences, but we each use these three levels of reality as a basis for making sense of the world and interacting with each other.

The INSIGHT Model of Communication uses our three levels of reality (facts, feelings, and meanings) as an intellectual structure we can use to communicate with and relate to each other. Facts allow us to talk about the world and our experiences in black and white. Feelings add in color, and meanings provide a third dimension and the context we need for genuine connection and intimacy.

Summoning the will and courage it took to overcome their fears and talk about these three progressively *deeper* levels of human experience changed these men. It happened over, and over, and over again. The model allowed them to overcome the prison code, establish clear personal boundaries, build genuine relationships, and discover beliefs and feelings they didn't know they had.

The Model

Level I: Revealing the Facts

Level I self-disclosures are information in nature and relate to ***objective reality***.

Level I self-disclosures require a commitment to stop lying or misleading other people.

Level I self-disclosures require ***honesty.***

Level II: Revealing Thoughts and Feelings

Level II self-disclosures require you to reveal your normally private internal ***subjective reality,*** including your thoughts and feelings.

Level II self-disclosures require you to recognize and honor your feelings *and* the feelings of others.

Level II self-disclosures exhibit ***empathy.***

Level III: Revealing Meanings

Level III self-disclosures *transcend* our ordinary, routine ways of communicating and require you share the *meaning* you have attached to your experience. This is referred to as ***inter-subjective*** reality.

Level III self-disclosures are the basis of ***intimacy.***

[One way to help you to understand the process is to give you a copy of the goals and objectives every member received when he joined the program.]

Group Guidelines

The primary objective of the INSIGHT Program is to learn to develop insight into your life crime, as well as, insight(s) into the person you have become since committing your life crime. In essence, the goal is to evolve and grow into the person you were meant to be by learning how to develop:

1) *critical thinking skills,*
2) *emotional intelligence,*
3) *advanced communication skills, and*
4) *INSIGHT*

<u>Critical Thinking Skills</u>
Critical thinking *involves asking certain "critical" questions designed to connect your thinking with your feelings.* Critical thinking *is different from...*

Analyzing
Ruminating
Pondering
Inspecting

In the *INSIGHT Program,* critical thinking means asking and answering these **Five (5) Critical Questions**:

1) **What's the issue?** *(What are the "facts"?)*
2) **What are you feeling?** *(Warriors honor their feelings!)*
3) **What are they feeling?** *(If uncertain... Ask!)*
4) **Whose drama is this?** *(People create dramas in their lives to get their emotional needs met.)*
5) **What if I change the meaning?** *(Changing meanings always changes the feeling!)*

[See chapter 3]

Emotional Intelligence

Emotional intelligence is related to being able to identify and honor your emotions, learning how to regulate and manage your feelings, and being able to effectively express yourself. In addition, it includes learning to notice and honor other people's feelings. Remember, people create the dramas in their lives to get their emotional needs met. If you cannot identify and honor your own feelings you won't be able to connect with other people, including those people on the parole board.

This will be your biggest challenge because the number-one thing people do in prison is to hide, deny, and avoid their feelings. They do this by "thinking" and using their thinking to avoid their feelings.

Group Guidelines

To succeed and stay in this group you must learn to speak in the "first person." That means starting your sentences with...

"I think..."
"I believe..."
"It's my opinion that..."

In addition, you need to learn to avoid over-using pronouns:

"He said..."   *("He" ... who?)*
"They..."   *("They"... who?)*

Remember, using the word "but" in a sentence negates everything that came before it.

"I'd like to apologize for my behavior, but..."
"I'd love to help you move, but..."

There are five (5) steps in using the **INSIGHT Model.**

> *Step 1: Ask and answer the* **Five (5) Critical Questions.**
> *Step 2: Decide whether to "***Act***" or "***Let it be.***"*
> *Step 3: If you decide to "***Act,***" then either share what you are feeling (empathy) or what something means to you (intimacy).*
> *Step 4: Seek to "***Dialogue***" whenever possible.*
> *Step 5: "***Let it go.***"*

Postscript

All good things must come to an end, and the *INSIGHT Program* came to an end in 2013. At that time, there were seventeen men still in the program. Within the next 3 years, fourteen of those men had either been released on parole, or had received their out dates. I have been able to stay in contact with most of them, including KK. Our conversations following their release were powerful reminders of the meaningful time we spent together and the energy and changes the *INSIGHT Program* generated.

In 2016, one ex-group member, Nate Williams, contacted me. Since his release, Nate has been speaking to numerous civic groups, community outreach programs, and youth organizations in the hopes he might prevent disenfranchised young men from following in his footsteps.

One of the people who learned about his efforts was Katherine Tebrock, Esq. She is the *deputy director of mental health-care services for the California Department of Corrections and Rehabilitation.* (Go figure!) At her invitation, Nate and I spoke about the *INSIGHT Program* to the *directors of the mental health programs* from each of the thirty-three prisons (thirty for men, three for women) in the CDCR.

The INSIGHT Program demonstrated to me that people can grow and learn to develop character and a sense of integrity. The men in the *INSIGHT Program* learned how to replace their *criminal thinking patterns* with the core beliefs and values of responsible human beings. I know this because I had the opportunity to work with each one of them, *personally.*

After living in oblivion and being almost completely forgotten for decades, these men are now faced with living and surviving in a very different world from the one they left. Here's a little peek into what it's like to have a second chance at life from someone just released after thirty-six years of confinement.

Hey Doc, how are you? I am doing just great, elated beyond belief!

I went into a thrift store and bought two tennis rackets for $5.00 and a yoga mat for 2 bucks! Oh, and the "99 Cent Store," don't get me started! I'll put it this way, they already know me by my name. I'm a preferred customer on a first name basis. And Google and Amazon... are you kidding me?

I start work next week. I got my first honest blister a week ago. I was doing some yard work out in the back yard here, mowing the yard, hoeing some weeds and pruning this lemon tree. I googled "How to Trim a Lemon Tree" and I tell you, 12 easy steps later I can enter it in a Better Homes and Garden Showcase. Google is amazing! It even taught me how to make a lemon pie... and it was good.

The house I'm staying at is fantastic. In the morning, I do my yoga at 5am under the early morning stars. It's so serene and peaceful. I can smell the lemons and rose bushes from the neighbors' yard. The quiet is so blissful my eyes well up with joy.

CHAPTER 3

The Five (5) Critical Questions

Imagine there are three people sitting in a large empty room. The first is a physicist, the second is an artist, and the third is a paranoid schizophrenic. The physicist is likely to be busy *visualizing* complex mathematical equations because that's what physicists do. The artist is likely to be *imagining* his or her next creation, and the schizophrenic is likely to be consumed in a world of inner *subjective* experiences and out of touch with the rest of the world.

Each one is *conscious*, and neurologically, all three people are engaged in using the same mental processes. *Intentionality* distinguishes the physicist and the artist from the schizophrenic. The difference between the actual experiences for each individual relates to who is in control of the process. The ability to choose what we focus our attention on and control our thinking is a function of the prefrontal cortex, and it's one of the things that separates human beings from other primates and other higher forms of life.

There's a delicate balance, however, between learning how to control our thinking (the physicist), learning how to pay attention to what we think and feel (the artist), and getting lost and consumed in the process (the schizophrenic). Creating an "observing awareness" *means* building a mental stage within your mind where you can examine your thoughts, feelings, and impulses before you act on them. That allows you to use the space between your ears to catch the pause between stimulus and response.

The men in prison I worked with struggled with controlling their criminal thinking patterns and violent behaviors. They spend their lives cycling in and out of jail, or prison. I've counseled other individuals who live in *virtual* prisons because of their limiting beliefs and fear of their own emotions. These people spend their lives trying to cope with living in their "self-imposed" prisons by avoiding their feelings. In each case, the individuals involved are dealing with the consequences of failing to learn how to control their thinking.

The **Five (5) Critical Questions** is a model of critical thinking originally developed for men in prison. In the heat of the moment, during a conflict, their self-destructive impulses very often take over and lead to violence. The **Five (5) Critical Questions** established a structure for them to use to control their impulsivity by controlling the thinking that precedes and often initiates their violence. The model accesses the *synergy* that comes from integrating your *conscious*, rational mind with your *unconscious*, intuitive body. The model has proven to be an effective method that anyone can learn and use to gain control of their thinking.

Asking and answering the **Five Critical (5) Questions** will reveal the largely *unconscious* beliefs you are using to understand the world and interact with other people. The goal is to develop and integrate an awareness of *both* your subjective and objective experiences. The model is based on the insight that our feelings are anchored to the meanings we have attached to an experience.

The Five (5) Critical Questions

(1) "What's the issue?" [This refers to the "facts" or your eye-witness account of what is happening.]

(2) "What are you feeling?" [We try to avoid or deny our feelings]

(3) "What are they feeling?" [If you don't know or can't guess, ask!]

(4) "Whose drama is this?" [Whose emotional needs are driving the conflict or situation?]

(5) "What if... I change the meaning?" [Changing meanings changes the underlying feeling.]

The Issue

The issue is a description or story about what is happening, or what has happened. It's one person's version of the "facts." Keep in mind, there is no one set of facts about anything. If there are ten eyewitnesses to an accident, there will be ten different sets of facts. Each person has a slightly different perspective and each person's version of what happened will be different from all of the other eyewitness accounts. No one perspective is the right perspective. Multiple points of view generate multiple sets of facts.

"The Issue" is what a video camera might capture if the conflict or incident in question were recorded. It lacks any emotional content or background information. It describes what is happening. Say, for example a husband forgets that today is his wife's birthday. In simple terms, "The Issue" is that a husband forgot that today is his wife's birthday.

The Drama

Most people are unaware of how repressed emotions influence our interactions with other people. Those unexpressed emotions *unconsciously* influence our decisions and determine the kinds of relationships we're capable of establishing. "The Drama" is using a relationship to act out your unmet emotional needs.

When two people meet and interact, there's a tendency for one or the other to try to take control of the conversation. "The Drama" is how one person attempts to get another person to defer to his or her model of the world. One of the most frequent dramas involves adopting a "Poor Me" attitude as a way to get attention, through *sympathy*. Social media provides an excellent example of the "Poor Me" drama with a phenomenon known as "humble bragging." Humble bragging is an attempt to camouflage a brag or a boast, as a complaint, by slipping in information designed to get *sympathy* from the other person.

These examples were taken off of Twitter @Humblebrag:

Totally walked down the wrong escalator at the airport from the flashes of the cameras. Go me!

It always feels a little odd to me when I get recognized randomly in public. I never know what to say. I'm glad it doesn't happen often.

I just did something very selfless. But more importantly, it was genuine & I know it meant a lot to the person in the long run.

Another popular drama is "The Critic." "The Critic" uses criticism to manipulate or control a conversation. "The Critic" sounds like this: "You know, those old clothes are so out of date, they make *you* look old"; or, "I've noticed that you tend to interrupt people when they're talking." The criticism can focus on how someone does his or her job, the way the person drives, or any number of personal characteristics. It doesn't matter. Anything will work as long as it is unsolicited, catches the other person off guard, and results in a moment of insecurity or self-doubt.

The purpose of the criticism is to establish the speaker as the ultimate judge and jury of how things should be. The speaker perceives him or herself to be a caring person, someone who pays attention to details and makes sure that things get done the right way. However, there is no one right or wrong way to do anything. We don't walk right foot, wrong foot.

A series of studies found these dramas to be attempts for validation and acceptance. Social media exposes feelings of insecurity in some people and some of those researchers reported that up to 75 percent of the people they studied suffered from FOMO (the fear of missing out).

Using the Five (5) Critical Questions

Events have no meaning until we give them meaning. In the example of the husband who forgot that today is his wife's birthday, "The Drama" includes the emotional reactions of the wife and the husband to his forgetfulness. The husband is likely to feel foolish, but his wife is far more likely to feel hurt or angry. The reason she feels different from her husband is that she has attached a different *meaning* to his forgetfulness than he has.

In his belief system, his forgetfulness *means* he can be a caring husband who does foolish things and is sometimes forgetful. However, in the wife's belief system, a husband who forgets his wife's birthday, is a husband who doesn't love his wife. Since *meanings* are always tied to feelings, if they can each learn to view the situation from a different perspective, it will change the meaning they have attached to his "forgetfulness." Finding common ground will alter the way each feels about the situation.

The men in the *INSIGHT Program* learned to use the model to break virtually every problem, conflict, or issue down into asking and answering the **Five (5) Critical Questions.** However, there were times in the heat of the moment, when the **Five (5) Critical Questions** would slip into the background, as their old reactive behaviors resurfaced. So, I developed the following mnemonic device for them to use when they were under stress.

R Review the model
E Emotions (yours and theirs)
L Look for INSIGHT
A Act don't react then
X Exit (let it go)

Review the model *means* recalling the first question:

What's the issue?

Emotions reference the next three questions:

What are you feeling?
What are they feeling?
Whose drama is this?

Look for INSIGHT means:

What if... I change the meaning?

Act... means *self-disclose* what you're feeling, or share the meaning you have attached to the situation.

X was a reminder to Exit or "Let it go."

The **Five (5) Critical Questions** model is an effective way to change the thinking patterns that lead to loneliness, depression, and anxiety. The primary goal of using the model is to expose the relationships between our thoughts and our feelings. That's where the insights are hidden.

If you find yourself struggling with a personal issue, the model can help you gain insight into your thinking and behavior. The most important thing is to question the *meaning* you have attached to the problem or situation. The insights come from being willing to consider a different point of view. Trust your intuition and challenge yourself to accept what you discover to be true.

Group Example

[IW was a founding member of The INSIGHT Program. He shared this story with the group as the turning point for him in learning how to understand and use the model.]

Early one morning, IW was in the bathroom shaving in the dark with the lights off, which had been his habit since he first came to prison. While he was shaving, another inmate came in and immediately turned the lights on. Reacting without speaking, IW turned the lights back off. The other inmate turned the lights back on, and then IW turned the lights back off. The second inmate turned the lights back on and said, "If you turn that light switch back 'on'… its 'On'"!

IW went back to his cell to put his boots on because that's what you do when there's going to be a fight. Sitting on his bunk, struggling with his boots, he noticed that his heart was pounding, and his head was spinning. In his head, he heard himself say, "Why is it always me that trouble finds?" In the very next moment, inside his head, he heard *my* voice say, "Use the model." So, he asked himself the **Five (5) Critical Questions**.

When he did, he remembered thinking: Wait a minute; this isn't about a light switch [The Issue]. That guy doesn't know I've always shaved in the dark because I can't stand looking at myself in the mirror. It reminds me of where I am and what I did to get myself here. At that moment, he also realized "The Drama" was his. That guy has no idea why I made such a big deal about that damn light switch. I'm frustrated and mad, and he's mad at me!"

He realized he had a choice.

He could react emotionally and go back in there and fight, which he had done many, many times in the past. Or, he could he could use the model and go back in there and share what that light meant to him. Because in the model, "Act" means communicate, not fight. To his credit, IW chose the high road. IW went back into that bathroom and said; "My bad! I can't stand looking at myself in the mirror because it reminds me of where I am, what I did, and how I screwed up my whole life. So, I've always shaved in the dark."

Instead of resorting to violence, IW said he remembered to **RELAX** and ask himself the **Five (5) Critical Questions**. That pause and insight gave him the opportunity to take control of his thinking and impulsivity. It also gave him the chance to use the communication skills he learned in the group. As a result, his self-disclosure was genuine, and his apology was sincere.

IW said the simple act of sharing what that light meant to him, changed him in profound ways (actually, he changed when he decided to use the model). He also shared that the experience was so powerful that it created a very personal relationship between two men who might otherwise have become bitter enemies.

Getting Unstuck

In the 1950s, it was a widely accepted fact that no one would ever run a sub four-minute mile. Then, in 1954, Roger Bannister ran one in three minutes, fifty-nine and four-tenths seconds. The very next year, *fifty* people broke the four-minute barrier. Today, high school athletes break it all the time. The truth is, any one of those fifty people could have figured that out on their own. They didn't need to wait for Roger Bannister to show them that the barrier wasn't real.

Your mind "runs" on questions, so you have to be especially careful about the questions you ask. The secret to getting unstuck and gain control of your thinking is learning how to ask yourself the right questions.

Learn to stop asking "why" (Why did you do that?). That question throws people into their minds and encourages rationalization. Rationalizing and defending yourself is not the same thing as expressing yourself. All of us have a plausible explanation for the things we do. Our reasons won't be accurate, however, because nobody really knows why they do anything.

There is a question, however, you can ask that will open up your mind and set you free whenever you feel stuck.

What if... I'm wrong?
What if... I'm right... but there's a better (easier) way?

Here are some more questions you can use to uncover some of the beliefs and values you're using to make your decisions and motivate your behaviors.

What happened?	*Objective*
How did you feel when "that" happened?	*Subjective*
What did it *mean* to you that... happened?	*Intersubjective*
What if you change the *meaning*?	*INSIGHTS*

CHAPTER 4

Mental Health?

Our current mental health-care system is based on the medical model of "mental illnesses." This model views all significant problems of thinking, feeling and behaving as being caused by brain or nervous system malfunction. This belief persists despite the fact that no "mental illness" has ever been linked to any neural pathology. We talk on and on about mental health, but we waste our time and money documenting and categorizing "mental illnesses." The people who support the medical model will try to convince you that human struggle is a brain disease.

The simple truth is that there has never been any scientific support for this belief. As early as the 1930s, psychiatrist Alfred Adler, a contemporary of Sigmund Freud and Carl Jung, advocated for a *holistic* model over the medical model. Adler believed if you want to help someone, you have to view his or her problems from within the context of his or her environment and see people as human beings rather than as a collection of symptoms.

Psychiatrist William Glasser, who created "reality therapy," eventually changed his whole concept of mental health. Glasser came to believe that the underlying cause of most mental health problems is unhappiness in our relationships with other people, not nervous system malfunction.

The original term for what we now call psychologists was "alienists." At the turn of the century, the insane were thought to be estranged or alienated from their normal faculties, so they needed an *alienist*. That's ironic because our current mental health-care system alienates us from our feelings. When mental health professionals ask people how many times they have been depressed in the last six months, they're sending an unconscious message that there's something wrong with being depressed.

The eminent psychiatrist R. D. Laing treated people with schizophrenia, and as an adult, he was himself hospitalized and treated for schizophrenia. His treatment method was highly successful but controversial. It involved no paid staff and no treatment. What Laing did was create living situations where the residents would learn to make friends with people they would otherwise avoid. This concept was based on Laing's observation that what these individuals needed, and craved most, were friendships and genuine connection with other people.

We Need a New Model

Each person's *subjective* experiences can be quite different, and each person's understanding and reactions to those experiences can be quite different as well. Everyone "hears" a voice inside his or her head and every artist uses his or her "visual hallucinations" to create the art that other people enjoy. What we currently refer to as "psychoses" are better understood and dealt with as examples of individual variability, rather than as evidence of a disease.

Symptoms and suffering are indications that something has gone wrong in a person's life, but they don't necessarily indicate the presence of a mental illness. Consider that people who live in countries with extreme levels of income inequality, as the United States, are *three times* more likely to suffer from *both* depression and anxiety. Virtually every psychotic experience is associated with someone's life problems, the most notable being family conflict and abuse.

The human brain is like a computer. It's a high-speed, multi-channel data analyzer that processes information. It also has software, like thoughts and ideas that are independent of the biological hardware of the brain. If the settings in an antivirus program are set to the max, the program may block e-mails from sources that aren't already in your address book. It might also ask you, *"Are you sure you want to visit this site?"* every time you try to visit a new site. From this perspective, a human being in crisis functions similar to an antivirus program with improper settings.

The program may be overly suspicious like someone diagnosed with schizophrenia. Or it may constantly check and re-check everything like someone diagnosed with an obsessive-compulsive disorder. Only a few of the settings have to be off for the computer, or the human being, to be dysfunctional.

From this perspective, hearing voices could be the result of setting the "loudness" scale too high. Similarly, paranoia could be the result of setting the "be careful" scale too high. There may be nothing wrong with the computer, or the human being; the problem might be that the program (the person's thinking) needs adjusting.

Honoring Our Emotions

It's not a good idea to put labels on our emotions and then try to avoid the ones we don't like. Our feelings contain information about the world inside our bodies, as well as, information about what's going on in the environment. Feelings aren't good or bad; our feelings are the body's way of communicating with us. Our feelings are also a critical part of our interpersonal communication.

As early as the 1940s, Wilhelm Reich proposed that cancer was the result of our failure to express our emotions. Reich was not only ridiculed by the medical and scientific communities; he was persecuted for his beliefs. In fact, he was the last man to be imprisoned by the United States government for his ideas. In 1956 all available copies of his life's work were rounded up and incinerated by the FDA. There is now evidence that Reich was right.

Dr. Candice Pert, the chief of brain biochemistry at the National Institutes of Health for thirteen years, wrote about Reich's ideas in *Molecules of Emotion*. In her book, Dr. Pert states, "Emotional expression is always tied to the flow of peptides in the body and the chronic suppression of emotions results in a massive disturbance of the psychosomatic network." That means the networks that connect the mind with the body can become so taxed from repressed emotions that the "molecules of emotion" become bogged down and can't flow freely. Stress-related diseases are examples of information overload not evidence of a "mental illness."

Music, art, and dance are universal ways of honoring and communicating feelings that words alone could never express. Willie Nelson is fond of saying that country music is "three cords and the truth." George Jones is known as the man who taught the world how to sing with a broken heart. His song, "He Stopped Loving Her Today" was voted the greatest country song of all time. Many people also consider it the saddest and the most beautiful love song of all time. George said he didn't want to record the song because he thought it was too sad, and he didn't think people would buy the record. Whenever I hear that song, I tear up and get a lump in my throat. Imagine all that coming from three cords and the truth.

Consider this: without depression we wouldn't have the *blues*; and without the *blues*, we wouldn't have rock 'n' roll, or the Beatles. In the early 1960s, a group of rockers, including Bob Dylan and Chuck Berry, fell in love with the *blues* music coming out of the local clubs in Chicago. They took lessons from bluesmen like Muddy Waters and Howlin' Wolf. Their experiences with these *blues* icons were the beginnings of rock 'n' roll.

To me, Dire Straits's "Walk of Life" is the *greatest* classic rock song of all time. When I hear that song, it touches my soul, and I feel sensations on my skin that researchers at Wesleyan College call "skin orgasms." At first, it was the driving beat and melody that got to me, but after I saw the video and understood the message, I think it should be the anthem for this book.

My wife, on the other hand, is highly passionate and very knowledgeable about classical music (I know, there's no accounting for taste). Her favorite piece of music is Mozart's Piano Concerto #21. When she listens to that concerto, it soothes her soul, and she experiences the "Mozart effect," which lowers her blood pressure and improves her concentration and work performance.

Symptoms or Failed Strategies?

Every problem must be viewed from the context in which it occurs. A strategy that proved successful at one point in time and under one set of circumstances may be entirely inappropriate and dysfunctional under another set of circumstances. As children, we dealt with frustration by crying and then waiting for someone to come and fix the problem for us. As adults, we learn that crying when we're frustrated won't fix the problem, and no one is coming to our rescue.

Instead of using context and our creativity to come up with solutions to our problems, we prefer the "work harder at what isn't working" approach. Instead of embracing the need to change, which can be difficult, it's much easier to keep repeating the same old behaviors over and over, even when they're not working. The medical model calls these repeating failed behaviors "mental illnesses."

In prison, men who are deemed "suicidal" are sent to the Mental Health Crisis Bed unit. As soon as they arrive, they're placed in an isolation cell, relieved of all their belongings (including their clothes), and given medications to help them control their suicidal thinking. Once they're isolated from the rest of the world and any meaningful activity or stimulation, they start reporting delusions, paranoia, and depression. This process occurs even if their original complaint was just a ploy to get out of the mainline and into the MHCB unit in the first place.

This perceptual isolation causes these men to mistake their self-talk as "voices." They misidentify the source of their thoughts as coming from outside their own bodies. Over time, they end up becoming dependent on psychotropic medications and cycling in and out of crisis bed units. Now, there's a failed strategy for you.

Here's the real problem. Anyone who has ever strolled down memory lane and imagined his or her childhood home, or heard the voice of an old friend, has seen things that aren't there and heard voices calling his or her name. Who says these universal *subjective* human experiences are symptoms of mental illnesses?

WHO Says?

The World Health Organization (WHO) claims that depression is a "global disease burden" and a "worldwide epidemic" that affects one out of every four people. WHO's statement simply reinforces what we already know. It's true that depression affects one out of four people, because depression affects everyone. Getting depressed is a part of life. The real question is, when do sorrow, unhappiness, and loneliness become depression, and according to whom?

Emotional pain is a necessary and essential part of life because it holds the keys to our personal growth. We have stigmatized a routine part of life by putting a label on it and calling it a "mental illness." Instead of learning how to honor our feelings, we have sanctioned ways to escape from them. This effort to avoid our uncomfortable feelings is evidenced by the fact that we consume over 80 percent of the painkillers and 60 percent of the psychiatric drugs prescribed in the world today.

According to the medical model, "mental illnesses" are permanent and continue throughout one's life. This belief just isn't accurate. Lots of people overcome their addictions and mental illnesses. Twenty percent of the soldiers fighting in Vietnam became addicted to heroin. Within one year of their return home, 95 percent of them stopped using heroin. Another study found that addicts who didn't receive any treatment at all were as likely to stop using drugs as those who went to treatment.

Study after study has shown that most people diagnosed with a "mental illness" recover without seeking treatment. Data from the University of Manitoba revealed that 50 percent of the five thousand participants they studied who had a diagnosis, no longer met the criteria at follow-up, without receiving any intervention or mental health care services. The idea that biological solutions are just around the next corner has no scientific basis. It's a firmly held and widely accepted belief that meets the criteria of a mass delusion.

Researchers at University College London found that the same symptoms used to diagnose and treat "mental illness" can manifest themselves in people after only *fifteen minutes* of exposure to isolation conditions. The subjects in the study started to crave stimulation, even talking, singing or reciting poetry to themselves to break the monotony. The researchers had hoped to observe their subjects over several weeks, but the trial was cut short because the volunteers became too distressed to carry on. Only a few lasted two days, and none lasted longer than a week.

The results of these studies shouldn't be that surprising, because we have known for a long time that other primates don't fare well in isolation. The most graphic examples come from work with rhesus macaque monkeys by psychologist Harry Harlow in the 1960s. Harlow deprived the monkeys of social contact after birth for months and even years. The monkeys became enormously disturbed after just thirty days. After a year, they were obliterated socially, incapable of social interaction of any kind.

Researchers in the 1970s set up two separate cages of rats. In one cage, a rat was left alone and isolated, so it couldn't touch or see other rats, and it had nothing to do to occupy its time. In the other cage, the rats had good food, running wheels, platforms for climbing, and lots of other rats to play with and have sex with. In both cases, the rats had access to two drinking bottles: a bottle of pure water and another bottle filled with morphine water (morphine is pure heroin). At the end of the day, the two bottles were measured. The rats in solitary confinement almost always picked the heroin water, and "Rat Pack" rats seldom drank the heroin water, and none became addicted.

People find refuge in whatever it is that takes away their pain. When people are trapped in a situation where their world becomes intolerable, and they feel there is no way out, they will leave mentally, even if they can't leave physically. Soldiers fighting in Vietnam, rats in solitary confinement and individuals in pain don't become victims of drugs, but of their environment. Addiction is one way of coping with being separated from everything that gives meaning to your life.

Today, when we find ourselves faced with a psychological or emotional crisis, we're encouraged to go and see a doctor. Based on unscientific assumptions, we're told that we suffer from a life long mental illness and will need to be on medications for the rest of our lives. Little attention is given to the nature of our interpersonal relationships or the relationship between the crisis and our current social situations.

It's diagnose, dose, and adios.

When we fail to give our brain direction, it will run on and on recycling old thinking patterns until we get bored, or sick, or until someone else finds a way to run it for us. We don't need more research into how many ways our lives can go wrong and be unhappy. It's time to embrace a *humanistic* model of mental health that acknowledges that our mental health and well-being is primarily dependent on our thinking, our beliefs and models of the world, and the nature of our relationships with other people.

CHAPTER 5

What's real?

I t was a revelation to me when I learned that space isn't really empty. In fact, what appears to be "empty" space is filled with *dark matter* and *dark energy*. Together, they make up over 90 percent of the matter in the universe. It's called *dark matter* because it neither emits nor reflects light or any other electromagnetic radiation. We still don't have any direct evidence of its existence, but Einstein demonstrated through a set of equations, that the mass of a star or planet distorts this *dark matter* and we experience this distortion as *gravity*.

Einstein's equations also showed that the universe is curved and distorted in an incredibly strange way. If we could travel in a perfectly straight line, in one direction over a great enough distance, we would return to the very same place we started. And that's not even the weirdest part of reality. The central lesson of quantum physics is this: there are no objective "things" sitting out there in space. Stars and planets, like particles of physics, have no objective, *observer-independent* features. That chair you're sitting on will cease to exist the moment there is no one around to perceive it.

Our experience of a world of separate things is a kind of optical illusion. What we see is a function of our physiology, not reality. As we dig deeper and deeper into the nature of reality, we find there is only an interconnected web of energy relationships. There is no single reality. There are no basic building blocks of nature and no atoms to smash. What we thought was real turns out to be a mystery.

Like someone chained to the wall of a cave, we can be clueless about how things work. Consider, as an example, our system of mandatory education. At the turn of the century, education was considered a branch of industry and an important part of the socialization process. The primary goal of socialization was to alienate children from their families, religions and other cultures so no counteracting influence could intervene. James Mill, the philosopher and founding father of classical economics, stated that the real purpose of mandatory education is to "train the minds of the people to a virtuous attachment to their government." In essence, the primary goal of mandatory education is to develop respect for authority. Talk about living in the dark.

The primary goal of socialization is to have you and me so dependent on the system that our behavior is predictable. The reason your local grocery store wants you to sign up for their mail-in rebates and weekly coupons isn't to save you money. The question, "Would you like to give us your ZIP code or phone number so we can tell you about our upcoming promotions?" is a lure. If you take the bait, you've been hooked. One way to confirm this is all those catalogs you get that you don't remember ordering and didn't pay for. What retailers really want to do is monitor our buying habits. They add that information to other publicly available information and then they sell that information to other businesses.

The combination of television and the mass media has created a socializing force so powerful almost none of us can escape its influence. Less than twenty-four hours after John Roberts was nominated to the Supreme Court, America Online conducted a poll. The poll asked people whether or not they thought he should be confirmed. Of the 113,085 people who responded, 47 percent said, "Yes"; 28 percent said, "No"; and 25 percent said they hadn't made up their minds yet. A shocking 75 percent of those polled had made up their mind in less than twenty-four hours, even before they had any information about him or his record.

Advertisers no longer waste their time developing intelligent ad campaigns. The advertising industry has learned that repeated exposure to even meaningless symbols will eventually create a sense of familiarity in buyers. It's known as the *mere exposure* effect. The "mere exposure" effect is so powerful that it has become the favored technique used to sell merchandise and services. It has also become the focus of virtually all political ad campaigns. At election time, voters are inundated with catchy little mini-ads that give us only the candidate's name and easy to remember sound bites.

We need to be aware that technology today isn't neutral. The people using this new technology are using proven neuroscience to create dependent behaviors. Those smart phones are now being engineered to be addictive. A handful of people at a handful of companies are shaping how one *billion* people think and feel every day with the choices they make with their phones. They call it "engagement"; I call it "brain hacking."

These people aren't evil, but they are definitely in a race to get to our brain stem, which is the seat of emotions like fear and anxiety. We check our cell phones for messages, on average, every fifteen minutes. Marketers use that knowledge to formulate an "addiction code" for the brain. They use algorithms to tell them precisely when to reward you. For instance, a "like" on Facebook that makes you want to come back for more. This technology will keep you in a continual state of anxiety. The long-term effects are unknown, but this behavior is ruining our relationships and our ability to focus.

The American Dream

The American Dream is a set of ideals including democracy, rights, liberty, opportunity, and equality. The dream promises the opportunity for prosperity, success, and upward mobility through hard work. Over time the dream expanded to include the belief that there are some wise men and women out there, making decisions and acting in our best interests. George Carlin said it best: "It's called the American Dream because you have to be asleep to believe it."

Here's the problem: the American Dream is an ideological carrot. Suggesting that America is a land of unlimited opportunities for success through hard work, is like suggesting the Pacific Ocean provides unlimited opportunities for swimming. They're both true statements. However, you better have the specific skills and abilities you need to succeed because opportunity and intention aren't going to be enough.

This county does an excellent job of creating wealth but a terrible job of distributing it. Almost 70 million Americans live in "hand-to-mouth" households, and one out of four of us has less than $250 in the bank on any given payday. We lag behind all European countries as well as Australia, Canada, Japan, and New Zealand with children living in poverty. It turns out that life outside the cave is a lot like life inside the cave mostly smoke and mirrors.

If the American Dream is unlimited opportunities for financial success, then the American Nightmare is debt. Most of us have little time for dreams because we've been worn down, beaten up, and are up to our eyeballs in credit-card debt. I know because I have been there. The only people talking about the American Dream are advertisers and politicians. And they're only interested in getting their hands on whatever money we have left. Part of the problem comes from the fact one out of five ex-cave dwellers say he or she would rather go to the dentist than spend a half-an-hour learning about money management.

Orwell's Problem

A man stumbles into a deep well and falls a hundred feet before he manages to catch hold of a tree root. When he looks up, all he can see is a small circle of blue sky. He begins to tire, and he realizes he's getting weaker and weaker by the moment. In desperation he cries out, "Is there anybody up there?" Suddenly the clouds part, a beam of light shines down on him and a deep voice thunders, "I, the Lord, am here. Let go of the root, and I will save you." The man pauses for a moment and then yells, "Is there anybody else up there?" If you can't trust the Lord, whom can you trust?

If you haven't figured out that the needs of the rich prevail over the needs of the not-so-rich, you must be living under a rock (or in a cave). If you haven't noticed the news media offers us only their biased views of the events they report, then you have to be sleep walking. And, if you don't know that the majority of us have been locked out of any meaningful role in the democratic process and our political system has been hijacked by the rich and powerful, then you're asleep at the wheel.

We start out our lives as self-reliant wonders, capable of incredible feats of learning and growth. Then a sophisticated social system slowly takes control of our thinking. The process eventually succeeds in alienating us from our innate self-reliance and leaves us gullible and predictable. If we're not alert, it comes at a high price because we become *self*-alienated strangers to ourselves.

The struggle to wake up, escape from the cave, and discover for ourselves how things work in the world is known as "Orwell's Problem." This is a reference to George Orwell's book *1984* (published in 1949), which is generally given credit for creating the basic framework for the kind of propaganda so prominent in the world today. In the book, Orwell uses techniques like *oversimplification* and *reversal of meaning* to install firmly held beliefs that are widely accepted but completely unsupported. The novel is a warning about the extremes people in power will go in order to manipulate and control our lives.

The Real World

In our struggle to determine what's real and what isn't real, there are people who think we aren't real. The premise is called the *simulation hypothesis*. The hypothesis is based on the idea that if there is some form of higher intelligence out there in the universe, then it's probably advanced enough to run simulations of worlds like our own. There could be trillions of realities, and we might be living in just one of them right now, but we're not aware of that.

The basic premise is this: we're living in a giant computer game being run by a far smarter civilization. Neil deGrasse Tyson, of the Hayden Planetarium, put the odds at fifty-fifty we're just illusions living in a make-believe world. That got me thinking. If I live in one of those realities and I don't like the one I'm in, can I transfer to another one and keep my '401(k)'?

Trying to answer the question "What's real?" is like trying to figure out how a three-pound lump of human tissue, obeying only the laws of physics, can give rise to *first-person* consciousness. That's known as the "Hard Problem" because things like brains, neurons, and neurotransmitters are just symbols we use to help us better understand how the nervous system works. They're not real. There is no three-pound lump of gray matter *either*. So, the brain I'm using to understand how my brain works doesn't really exist, and everything my brain conjures up is an illusion. Every time I try to use that logic to solve the "Hard Problem," I get dizzy.

Donald D. Hoffman is a professor of cognitive science at UC Irvine. He has spent three decades trying to solve the "Hard Problem" by studying perception, artificial intelligence, evolutionary game theory, and the brain. His conclusion is this: the world presented to us by our perceptions is nothing like reality. As a *conscious realist,* he postulates our *experiences* are what he calls the real "coin of the realm."

Our everyday experiences of life *my* feeling of a headache, *my* taste of cherry pie, and *my* feelings are the true nature of reality. Everyone's reality is as real as the next person's, only different. The only things that are real are my experiences for me, and your experiences for you.

CHAPTER 6

Who's real?

So, the answer to our question, "What's real?" is that the only true *reality* is the one we create for ourselves. Our personal experiences are the "coin of the realm" and the only true reality. My experience with trying to answer the question, "Who's real?" has been this: we are habitual concealers of ourselves. If asked, most people say they use language to express themselves and communicate with other people. My experience is different. I think a little self-reflection and honesty will convince you that we use language to:

1) **Play our roles and maintain our facades,**
2) **Manipulate others to get what we want, and**
3) **Establish and maintain a "safe" emotional distance from each other.**

Because we use language to create images of ourselves and maintain a "safe" emotional distance from each other, we have become intimate strangers. *Intimate* in the sense that we work and live near each other, but *strangers* because we keep our genuine thoughts and feelings hidden from each other. Even within our own families we keep secrets and avoid talking about certain uncomfortable topics. Have you ever tried to talk about politics, or your sexual hang-ups at your parents' house?

There are some places we just don't go.

To maintain and protect our facades, we will even try to ignore our feelings. If I'm afraid I can't handle the truth, I will try to ignore my feelings because feelings reveal the truth. Maintaining a "safe distance" from our emotions is a trap. The more comfortable we get with ignoring our feelings, the more indifferent we get to the feelings of others. I learned this lesson the hard way.

Even though we lie, deceive and mislead each other, we tend to behave in very predictable ways because we have all learned how to dance around the truth. Even when we change partners, we somehow manage to find someone whose need for a certain amount of emotional distance matches our own.

If we were truly using language to communicate with each other, then the Internet, Facebook, blogging, texting, and twitter should be providing us with endless opportunities to connect with each other. Instead, these technological advances have created new roles for us to play and more creative ways for us to hide from each other. In 2012, a Heisman Trophy candidate admitted he had an online relationship with a nonexistent woman. He said he lied about it because he was afraid he would be perceived as crazy for having a serious relationship with a woman he had never met.

One girl on Facebook claimed to have 468 friends; another fourteen-year-old girl ran up a mobile phone bill of $6,000 texting photos to her friends while she was on vacation in New York City. Texting trivial information about how you spend your time to people you may know only casually through the Internet is a good example of how deeply superficial our lives have become.

So, you've got fifty people on your Twitter account. Guess what, the Dalai Lama has eight million followers, and he doesn't even own a computer. The illusion is we're more interconnected than ever, but the reality is we're using these *virtual* relationships to avoid the honesty and hard work it takes to develop authentic relationships.

The anonymity of the Internet lures some people to edit out certain aspects of their personalities they would prefer to hide. Leaving out uncomfortable truths allows you to run from your problems, deny emotions you don't want to feel, and avoid things you would prefer to forget. This leads you back into the cave, and when you chain yourself to the wall of a cave, it's hard to meet new people. And, who wants to visit an old friend when it's a painful ordeal?

Almost everyone agrees that emotional connection is a critical part of our mental health, but there's a delicate balance between our need for intimacy and our fear of it. We want it, but we're afraid of it. In this culture today staying married to the same person for a lifetime qualifies as an alternative lifestyle. Even when two people stay together, they often do so for the kids, so they'll have an ear to talk into and have someone to control, or so there will be somebody around when they want to have sex. Our fear of intimacy results in overly cautious behaviors and avoidance of the truth. Instead of forging genuine relationships we settle for pseudorelationships, or "arrangements."

In an arrangement, the individuals involved silently conspire to avoid talking about, dealing with, or addressing certain uncomfortable topics. If you don't bring up my drinking, my laziness, or the way drive, I won't complain about your weird friends, the way you dress, or your stinky feet.

Many people confuse intimacy with *enmeshment*. Intimacy requires honesty, self-disclosure and the kind of communication skills not many of us have learned. Enmeshment is inappropriate caring for others (invading someone else's boundaries) and inappropriate reliance on approval from others (having weak personal boundaries). It's not wise to intervene in the lives of other people, but enmeshed people do it all the time. Enmeshed people say things like: "Let me help (control) you." They worry a lot about what other people should be doing and are overly concerned with what's best for other people.

How can you tell if you're in an arrangement?

An arrangement can look like a relationship. The two people involved might spend a lot of time together, they have probably met each other's families and friends, and other people might even refer to them as a couple. Arrangements, however are subtle struggles for control. Here are some clues that you might be in an arrangement and not a relationship:

1) **You find yourself having the same old arguments.**
2) **You can't or won't tell each other the truth.**
3) **There's a constant struggle to decide who's "right."**
4) **All of your efforts to help your partner (to change) have failed.**

Settling for arrangements means we never get to know each other or ourselves. That's because we can't reveal ourselves, to ourselves. The fundamental way we learn about ourselves is through honest interaction with other people. We need the honest feedback of others to overcome our self-deception and lack of perspective.

At some level, we're all aware of how much we dodge, deceive and avoid the truth, but we tacitly agree not to bring this up or talk about it. The pressure to avoid discussing our penchant for selecting pretense over authenticity can be so strong that some people will marry a complete stranger before they will commit to being open and honest about what they think and feel. In the end, they can find themselves married to an illusion composed of their fantasies and unmet emotional needs instead of a real person.

Healthy Relationships

Couples were divorcing at such high rates in the 1970s; there was a lot of concern about the impact these divorces might have on the children. Psychologists John and Julie Gottman have spent the last forty-two years helping couples build and maintain healthy relationships based on what they have learned about healthy relationships. By observing couples when they interact, the Gottmans can predict with a *94 percent accuracy* whether a couple will be broken up, together and unhappy, or together and happy several years later.

The Gottmans hooked couples up to electrodes and then asked them to talk about their relationship. They asked them questions about how they met, details of a major conflict, and details about a positive memory they each had. As they spoke, the electrodes measured each individual's blood flow, heart rate, and the amount of sweat they produced. From their data, the Gottmans separated the couples into two different groups: the "Masters" and the "Disasters."

The "Masters" were still happy and together after six years. They had low physiological arousal and their physiology remained calm. This calmness translated into warm, affectionate behavior.

The "Disasters," on the other hand, had either broken up or were chronically unhappy in their marriages. They appeared to be calm during their interviews, but their physiology told a different story. Their heart rates were rapid, their sweat glands were active, and their blood flow increased. They showed all the signs of being in "fight-or-flight" mode. This response sent their heart rates racing and made them more aggressive toward each other.

Simply having a discussion while sitting next to each other was like facing a dangerous situation. Even when they were talking about mundane or even pleasant aspects of their relationship, they were on guard against being attacked and prepared to attack. The data revealed that the more *physiologically* active the couples were in the lab, the quicker their relationships deteriorated over time.

One of the most important things the Gottmans found was that partners make "invitations to connect," or "bids," from each other. For example, my wife loves flowers and gardening. One day she notices a new flower is about to bloom. She might say something like, "Look at this beautiful little rosebud" (my wife does say things like that). She's not just commenting about the new rosebud. She's looking for a response from me, an opportunity for us to *emotionally* connect, even for just a moment, about the new flower.

This *flower bid* drama might seem minor, but it holds the secret to the health of the relationship. I must decide on a response to her "bid." My wife thought the flower was important enough to bring it up, and the question is, do I recognize and respect that? I can either "turn toward" her and show interest and engage with her; or I can "turn away" from her and continue doing whatever I was doing before her invitation to connect.

The Gottmans found that couples who stay together for more than six years have "turn-toward" responses 87 percent of the time. Couples who got divorced after six years had "turn-toward" responses 33 percent of the time.

In healthy relationships, couples are very respectful about the way they handle problems. They don't armor up and leap into battle. They're very sensitive and considerate.

It's not so much what someone discloses when he or she speaks, but how you respond to their self-disclosure that matters most. If you want to have an intimate relationship that will withstand the test of time, you need to be able to reconnect after experiencing a conflict. The most effective reconnections rely on reestablishing emotional connections rather than scoring intellectual victories.

It's the quality of your friendship that matters most. Be responsive, demonstrate to the other person you understood what he or she said. In the end, love is a working partnership and marriage requires learning how to communicate effectively on important issues.

The Internet Paradox

Researchers have found that *increased* Internet usage correlates with *increased* loneliness. Since it's only a correlation, we can't say whether or not the Internet makes people lonely, or whether lonely people are attracted to the Internet. I know this, though: it can be lonely, wandering the network of pseudofriends, trying to decide what part of yourself you want to share, who will listen, and what he or she might think. The bottom line is, it's like your mother always told you: you get out only what you put in.

It's hard to view people as real when so many people perform for an audience. John Cacioppo is the world's leading expert on loneliness. He found that Internet communication allows for only *pseudo*intimacy. Surrogates can never make up completely for the absence of a real, in-the-flesh person.

Cacioppo concluded that the greater the proportion of face-to-face interactions, the less lonely you are; and the higher the proportion of online interactions, the lonelier you are. The connections we make through the Internet are not the connections that bring us closer together; they're the connections we use to keep us preoccupied. And those individuals who are the most preoccupied are the most likely to browse sites that reinforce their current views.

Using Language to Communicate

Learning to use language to express yourself and communicate with other people requires a fundamental shift in your thinking. To begin, it means knowing the difference between self-disclosure and self-presentation. Self-presentation is using what you say to get a particular response from the person you're addressing. Unfortunately, this is what most people use language to do. Self-disclosure, on the other hand, is sharing your normally private internal *subjective* experiences, including your thoughts, feelings, and beliefs, with no attempt to influence or manipulate the other person.

The "facts, feeling, and meanings" model (see chapter 2) allows you to express yourself truly. Learning to speak in the *first person* ("I" think, "I" feel, or "I" believe) gives you the opportunity to uncover your core beliefs and discover things about yourself you didn't know were true.

The facts represent honesty and life in black and white, feelings add in color and *empathy,* and meanings add the context and perspective we need to develop genuine *intimacy.* It's not trust, but the courage to be honest and be ourselves that establishes intimacy and builds healthy relationships.

Feelings are our bodies' way of sharing information about what is going on in our lives, *both* internally and externally. The human brain is organized and skilled at interpreting this information and attaching meaning to it. The critical insight is that our feelings are tied directly to the meaning we have attached to an experience. Changing meanings allows you to develop awareness and the opportunity to connect your thinking with your feelings.

There's nothing that compares to intimacy for being a catalyst for self-discovery and growth. Intimacy is a life-enhancing experience and the elixir of life. All you have to do to experience intimacy is eliminate any dishonesty, drop all of your pretenses, and accept what *you* know to be true.

CHAPTER 7

Are You for Real?

Are you that person inside your head, the one you spend the majority of your time with, or are you the person saying all the right things and obeying all the rules that everyone else thinks you are? Some of our great philosophers, most cherished poets, and brightest social scientists have tried to answer that question. In fact, the struggle with the question, "Who am I?" has been referred to as the "Human Dilemma." In essence who are you when there's no one around to impress and no roles to play, who are you then?

I think the best answer to that question comes from psychoanalyst and writer Rollo May. In May's view, our "self" is an ongoing *process* rather than a fixed entity. Since we can experience ourselves both *objectively* and *subjectively*, the "self" emerges as a property of the oscillation between these two points of view. However, instead of a simple answer to our question, we're now faced with even more confusion. That's because answering the question "Who am I?" is an enigma, a puzzle to solve. The answer is we're *both* the person inside our head *and* the person playing social roles. It's not an *either/or* proposition because we're both, *simultaneously*, and so is everyone else.

The "Human Dilemma" is a delicate balancing act of accepting and playing our roles while at the same time, honoring our integrity and sense of individuality. You lose your balance whenever you sacrifice that part of you that makes you unique. No one ever started out life with the hope of living out someone else's dreams, and no one who ever accomplished anything great aspired to be just another one of the guys.

Lots of people talk about getting real, but stepping out of our roles and dropping our facades is a frightening thought. That's because we're all secretly afraid of being exposed for the frauds we are. Are you being genuine and honoring your true thoughts, feelings, and beliefs? Are you doing your own thinking, or are you waiting for someone else to tell you what to do?

The Hero's Journey

In mythology, a hero is someone who sees a crisis as a call to adventure. He or she resolves the crisis and then returns home a transformed human being. American mythologist Joseph Campbell was a great historian of the "hero's journey." For Campbell, the concept of a hero's journey is also a metaphor for our personal, spiritual, and psychological growth.

In 1931 Campbell traveled to California where he met and became good friends with budding writer John Steinbeck. While living on the Monterey Peninsula, both Campbell and Steinbeck fell under the spell of a marine biologist/philosopher named Ed Ricketts. They both started writing novels with Ricketts as the "hero"; however, unlike Steinbeck, Campbell never completed his book.

Steinbeck used Ricketts as the model for many of the characters in his great books. Ricketts was the inspiration for "Doc" in *Cannery Row*, for "Doc Burton" in *Dubious Battle*, and for "Jim Casy" in *The Grapes of Wrath*.

Ricketts was part sinner and part saint. He was comfortable with intellectuals as well as with the prostitutes and bums of Monterey's Cannery Row. This is how Steinbeck described Ricketts: "He wears a beard, and his face is half Christ and half satyr, and his face tells the truth." Steinbeck said Ricketts had a Zen-like acceptance of things as they are. He viewed him as a man in search of the ultimate goal, the *truth*.

Henry Miller, the American writer who wrote *The Tropic of Cancer* also wrote about Ed Ricketts. He wrote that Ricketts was "a most exceptional individual in character and temperament, a man radiating peace, joy, and wisdom. Satisfied with his lot, adjusted to his environment, happy in his work, and representative of all that is best." The whole world loves the rugged individual who is genuine, who stands up for what he believes, and isn't afraid to be himself.

I think a clue into what made Ricketts such a compelling person can be found in his writings. Here's an excerpt of his work where he compares man's social structure to life in a tide pool: "A study of animal communities has this advantage: they are merely what they are, for anyone to see who will and can look clearly; they cannot complicate the picture by worded idealisms, by saying one thing and being another; here the struggle is unmasked, and the beauty unmasked."

Steinbeck eventually became best friends with Ricketts. Together, they journeyed four thousand miles in a chartered fishing boat to the Gulf of California. On that trip, they discovered thirty-five new marine species and co-authored a book, *Sea of Cortez*. They were planning to travel to British Columbia and write another book, but one week before they were scheduled to leave, Ricketts was hit and killed by a train near Cannery Row. In *Cannery Row*, Steinbeck left behind this epitaph: "Doc would listen to any kind of nonsense and change it for you into a kind of wisdom. His mind had no horizon, and his sympathy had no warp."

The Human Element

I believe every person is imbued with a certain amount of "human element." This *human element* is a unique form of energy and is unlike any of other elements in the periodic chart of elements. That's because this *human element* is like dark energy and dark matter; we can't see it, touch it, or put in a bottle so we can study it, but we can feel it. In spite of the fact that we can't see this *human element*, I think it exerts a force that we experience as our *human spirit*.

Now, I'm no Einstein, so I don't have any fancy equations to support my theory, but I think this human element functions as a sort of social currency. When we allow other people to overly influence what we say or do, it depletes our human element. On the other hand, when we stand up for what we believe, we replenish our reserve of human element.

Nobody can take someone else's human element from him or her, but we too easily give away our human element when we sell ourselves short, give up on our dreams, and forget to honor what makes us unique. As a consequence, we lose a bit of our true nature and experience feelings of alienation and depersonalization.

This human element needed a proper scientific name, so I followed the established protocol. I looked to see how the last three most recently discovered elements received their names. Here's what I found: *moscovium* (Mc) was named for Moscow; *tennessine* (Ts) was named for the state of Tennessee; and *nihonium* (Nh) was named for Japan, where the element was first discovered (Nihon is how you say "Japan" in Japanese). Using what I learned from that, I concluded the proper name for this human element would be "*humanium*," and the correct symbol would be (Hm).

There was a time in our lives, when we were brimming with *humanium*, and our dreams mattered. Before we learned to become dependent on others, we approached life in our own unique way. Too young to listen to reason, we had the initiative and courage we needed to be ourselves. Without any training, we taught ourselves how to walk and talk, as well as the rules of the culture we adopted. Despite repeated failures and adversity, our *humanium* allowed us to maintain our focus and motivation to learn from our mistakes and persist over extended periods of time. Research has shown that our level of *humanium* and human spirit is a better predictor of success than IQ, or any other measure, when it comes to achieving long term success.

Nowhere Man

A life of lowered expectations, alienation, and isolation are the main themes in Erich Fromm's *Escape From Freedom* and Albert Camus' *The Stranger*. Both stories focus on a man who is a stranger in his own world. Fromm described him as "Nowhere Man." The Beatles also wrote and sang about Nowhere Man:

> Doesn't have a point of view
> knows not where he's going to,
> isn't he a bit like you and me?
> He's blind as he can be, just sees
> what he wants to see,
> Nowhere Man can you see me at all?

The loneliness, isolation, and alienation so characteristic of "neurosis" have spread into our culture as a whole. We no longer strive to do our very best. Instead, we're satisfied with working just hard enough to put ourselves somewhere in the middle of the pack. I call this the, "No need to be the *fastest* to survive, I just need to be faster than my *slowest* friend," strategy.

In a short story called "A Painful Case," James Joyce the Irish novelist and poet, wrote about Mr. Duffy. For James, Mr. Duffy is a "nowhere man who lived a short distance from his body." In the story, Mr. Duffy is a one-dimensional bureaucrat who works in a bank. His life is dull and boring because he has cut himself off from his feelings. His life lacks any purpose, and he has no meaningful relationships. He is known only by the rules he lives by and the roles he plays.

Do you know Mr. Duffy? He's that guy who's maxed out his credit cards, but he keeps finding ways to spend money he doesn't have. He doesn't care about his job, so he spends most of his time engaged in endless diversions. He fantasizes about winning the lottery as the solution to his problems and empty life. He looks like he has ignored his body for way too long and he's lost and doesn't know it. When he looks in the mirror, all he sees is a spare tire and a shocking number of wrinkles staring back.

Our Search for Meaning

How can we avoid becoming a "Nowhere Man," lost in the struggle just to survive? The answer comes from lessons learned in some of the most inhumane and oppressive conditions human beings have ever faced from the Nazi death and extermination camps, Auschwitz and Dakar. Viktor Frankl was a psychiatrist who survived internment in these death camps. Frankl was prisoner number 119,104, and he spent the majority of his time moving dirt and laying railroad tracks.

Frankl wrote about what he learned in a great book, *Man's Search for Meaning*. One of the themes in Frankl's book is that we are each challenged to find meaning in our lives, and each stage of our development requires a different meaning. As children, we find meaning in our families. As teenagers, we start to look outside the family for meaning while trying to discover who we are as people. As young adults, we typically find meaning in our work and our careers. At middle age, we begin to come to grips with our mortality; and toward the end of our lives, we tend to reflect on what we did, or did not do, with our lives.

If we successfully find meaning in each of these stages, we evolve and grow. Getting stuck, however, in one stage or another can cause loneliness, unhappiness and depression. If we reach a point of *apathy*, which Frankl described as "emotional death," it means we have forgotten that a difficult challenge provides us with the opportunity to grow.

Frankl believed there are three ways we can find or establish meaning in our lives. The *first* is by creating something or doing something for others; the *second* is through love; and the *third* way is through facing suffering head on. When we face suffering head on, we still suffer, but we maintain the will to fight. Frankl referred to this as the "defiant power of the human spirit." I believe this "defiant power" is Frankl's description of maintaining our human spirit and level of *humanium* by finding a purpose, or meaning for our lives. It's the fuel we need to be self-reliant and the secret behind our mental health and well-being.

My question for you is this: when your goal is to fit in and be like everyone else, are you measuring up or dumbing down?

CHAPTER 8

I feel, therefore I'm real

Did you know you can have as many as sixty thousand thoughts in a single day? This largely unconscious flow of ideas reflects the beliefs and values you have formed about the world. However, the number of thoughts you have in a day is not as important as understanding there is an underlying pattern to your thinking.

Ninety percent of the thoughts we have in a day are the same thoughts we had the day before.

This repetitive pattern of thinking is how we establish and maintain a concept of our "self" from one day to the next. It also explains why someone who suffers from paranoia doesn't go to bed one night and wake up the next morning and *forget* to be paranoid. The problem is that thinking distorts reality. An over reliance on our thinking means we have put our feelings on hold and ignoring your intuition is a slippery slope.

Too much thinking can cause anxiety which is the result of applying logical reasoning to an irrational fear. This excessive worry can get transmuted into physical symptoms. Anxiety can manifest itself into stomachaches, headaches, limb pain, and a general malaise that mimics mononucleosis and the flu. Primary-care physicians report that anxiety drives more people into their offices than the common cold does. Our thinking can become so automatic it can drop below our conscious awareness. When this happens, something is missing, and that something is...**you!**

Beliefs

If you raise fruit flies in a bell jar for just two days, and then remove the lid, 99.99 percent of those flies will remain trapped inside the bell jar. The reason the flies don't escape is they have made a *premature cognitive commitment* about the nature and extent of their world. Once they commit to the belief that their world ends where the lid begins, they never test that belief again. Because they never test that belief again, they remain trapped inside the bell jar for the rest of their lives.

Beliefs are phenomenal things. Our belief systems influence what we think and how we behave. Many of our beliefs are "mapped" onto us by our families and the culture around us and, for the most part, are *unconscious* and *unexamined*. A belief can drive someone to go out and do any number of irresponsible things, including murder, because of an idea. Understanding someone's belief system, however, doesn't help us predict what he or she might do. That's because we tend to be highly selective about our beliefs. For example, you have to be nice to me, but I don't have to be nice to you.

Values are *super*-beliefs infused with emotion. Once we become emotionally vested in our beliefs, our thinking becomes susceptible to "perceptual bias." Now, we no longer perceive things as they are, but rather as we believe them to be. A good example of *perceptual bias* comes from Rutgers University, and it's Robert Wood Johnson Medical School.

The medical school uses old episodes of the *Seinfeld* show to help medical students identify and discuss psychiatric disorders. Third- and fourth-year medical students begin rounds every morning by discussing which psychopathology is featured on certain episodes. Dr. Anthony Tobia, an associate professor of psychiatry explains their rationale: "You have a very diverse group of personality traits that are maladaptive on the individual level. Jerry's obsessive compulsion traits combined with Kramer's schizoid traits, with Elaine's inability to forge meaningful relationships and with George being egocentric" (yada, yada, yada).

In 2002, TV Guide named *Seinfeld* the greatest television show of all time. A television show "about nothing" was great because it was funny and people could see themselves and their own lives in the plot lines. Add in a little *perceptual bias*, and they become teaching tools for "mental illnesses." Jerry might be a smart ass, up-tight clean freak, but he's funny. Elaine's struggles are familiar to anyone who has ever been lonely and looking for love. Kramer is odd, like a lot of people, only transparent and harmless. And George is anxious, self-alienated, and insecure like the rest of us.

After coaching from Tobia, however, the medical students focus their attention on Dr. Tobia's biased views, and this creates a self-fulfilling prophecy known as "belief perseverance." Instead of turning our insecurities into pathology, the medical school could be using these old episodes as teaching tools for the health benefits of laughter on *both* our immune systems and our mental health.

Your Chemical Brain

Rene Descartes was the founding father of modern medicine and is probably best known for his statement, "Cogito ergo sum," or "I think, therefore I am." Descartes believed our ability to reason is independent of the body, independent of cultural influences and even separate from our self-interest. This Cartesian thinking divided human experience into two separate and distinct factions, the *mind* and the *body*. This separation set the tone for Western scientific thinking for the next two hundred years.

For decades, we have viewed the brain and the central nervous system as an electrical communication system. This was due primarily to the fact we only had tools that allowed us to see and study the electrical brain. We now have the tools we need to observe what is called the "chemical brain." As a result, we're now in the midst of a paradigm shift with major implications for how we think about health and disease.

Just like our eyes, ears, nose, tongue, fingers, and skin act as sense organs, receptors located in the membranes of our cells also function like sense organs. These receptors hover, dance and vibrate and pick up messages carried in the fluids that surround each cell. Once a receptor receives a message, it can transmit it from the surface of the cell into the cell's interior, where the message can dramatically change the state of the cell. This "chemical brain" is now considered to be a second nervous system.

Intelligence is located in cells throughout our body, not just in the brain. The *human immune system*, just like the *human nervous system*, has memory and the capacity to learn. The physiological and psychological processes that underlie our ability to reason are neither of the body nor the brain. They function as a coordinated whole. The phenomenon we refer to as the mind is the product of a structural and functional ensemble and not just from the brain. This means the separation of *mind* and *body* is not valid. Descartes was wrong; we can't separate the mind from the body.

Emotions

Your *body* is now considered to be your *subconscious mind*. Cells throughout your body, including cells from the endocrine, nervous, gastrointestinal, and immune systems all communicate with each other. You and your body are having an ongoing conversation, and the language they speak is called *emotions*. Most of the information they share is kept in order by our *chemical brain* and not by the synaptic connections of nerve cells.

Our *chemical brain* is older, more essential, and operates over much greater distances. "Intuition" is the experience of your body trying to have a conversation with you about important changes going on *both* inside and outside your body. The nervous system uses your five senses to monitor these changes, and these *internal* changes become the physiological basis of your emotions.

This sensory information gets transmitted to the brain where it is interpreted and evaluated. These evaluations become the *psychological* basis of your feelings. When you ignore or deny certain emotions because they make you feel uncomfortable, you lose access to that information, and you are the poorer for it.

Trying to ignore a feeling never really works anyway. Our emotions leak though in universal facial expressions that speak louder than words. Even children who are blind from birth have the same facial expressions as children who can see. When you're angry, pretending not to be angry doesn't mean you're not angry. Your heart rate, respirations, and body temperature will all increase because you're not just angry; your body is preparing itself for a fight.

Our emotions are connected to the *autonomic nervous system,* or the ANS. The *sympathetic branch* puts us on alert and prepares us for action. As that reaction subsides, the *parasympathetic branch,* the energy conserving system, takes over and returns the body to its baseline state. It's the body's way of reacting to any perceived threat, evaluating the threat, and then returning to its baseline state.

Understanding how the two branches of the ANS *naturally* work together can help you develop powerful insights and learn how to understand and manage your emotions. For example, the internal physiological state for *fear* and *excitement* are identical. The only thing that differentiates *fear* from *excitement* is our *subjective* evaluation of the situation. Each person on a roller coaster ride experiences the same ride, only different. Some people are "scared to death" and others are "high on speed." The underlying physiology is the same for each of these two very different experiences.

There is a theory, called the Opponent Process Theory of emotions, that hypothesizes that our emotions come in pairs. When we experience one member of the pair, referred to as A, it triggers an *opposite* emotion, or B, which has the effect of negating the first emotion. This functions to return the nervous system back to its original state. This process mirrors how the two branches of the ANS naturally work together.

$$\text{Baseline} \longrightarrow A \longrightarrow B \longrightarrow \text{Baseline}$$

Consider, for example, that you are about to make your first ever skydive, so you can scratch it off your bucket list. As you sit there contemplating what you're about to do, you're going to be a little conflicted about how you're feeling. On the one hand, you're excited, but you're a little nervous and anxious on the other. This model predicts precisely that. Your fear will automatically trigger the excitement or euphoria that comes with a successful jump. To take that leap of faith, your curiosity and excitement will have to prevail over your anxiety and fear.

Once you take that step, the longer it takes for the parachute to open, the more your fear will increase. The instant the parachute opens, however, your evaluation of the situation will change, and so will the way you are feeling. Your fear will transform instantly into euphoria the moment you see that parachute open safely. You're still under the effects of the adrenaline rush, but your *evaluation* of the situation has changed. It's the drama of *The Agony and the Ecstasy* played out in real time and in the *first* person.

The suggestion that our emotions are paired together as opposites is in harmony with the way the human nervous system operates. The balance between *excitation* and *inhibition,* the *endorphin* responses to *pain,* and the *color and negative afterimages* in the eye all involve a balance between opposing systems. When you reflect on it, this balance of opposites plays itself out in life: our reference to something being *bitter sweet,* fear and excitement, pleasure and pain, mass and energy, subject and object, even life and death.

A study from the Massachusetts Institute of Technology (MIT) found there are two separate populations of neurons in the *amygdala,* which is responsible for processing positive and negative emotions. These neurons are *genetically* programmed to encode memories of either fearful or pleasurable events. The researchers at MIT also discovered that one set of neurons can inhibit the other. When they stimulated activity in the "reward" neurons, activity in the "fear" neurons were suppressed, and vice versa. This is strong support for the "opponent process" theory.

A related study involved what are called "wrong" emotions for instance, the "tears of joy" of a crying spouse at seeing his or her loved one return home from war, or an athlete breaking into tears after scoring the winning basket or goal. The study found that people who express negative reactions to positive news were able to moderate their intense emotions more quickly. They also found evidence that strong *negative* feelings can provoke *positive* expressions for example, the nervous laughter you see in people confronted with a difficult or frightening situation.

No Feeling No Empathy

Some people can lose their ability to feel. People who have suffered certain types of damage to the *prefrontal cortex* make poor decisions and have little or no feeling. They stop showing respect for social rules, and the decisions they make don't take into account their own best interests. We might summarize their dilemma as knowing, but not feeling.

There is a neurological condition called "anosognosia," which is the lack of insight or awareness. It's also referred to as the inability to acknowledge a disease in oneself. A good example comes from Supreme Court Justice William O. Douglas who suffered a stroke in the right hemisphere of his brain in 1975.

Douglas knew that in 95 percent of all people, language depends primarily on left hemisphere structures. Douglas used that knowledge to argue for his return to the bench following his stroke. He not only checked himself out of the hospital against his doctor's advice, he also dismissed his *left*-sided paralysis as a myth, and he explained his hospitalization as the result of a fall.

When he was forced to admit, in an open press conference, that he couldn't walk or get out of his wheelchair unaided, he dismissed the matter by saying, "Walking has very little to do with the work of the Court." When asked a question about his leg he replied, "I've been kicking forty-yard field goals with it in the exercise room." He said he might even consider signing up with the Washington Redskins.

The stunned visitor countered that his age might put a damper on his plan. The justice laughed and said, "Yes, but you ought to see how I'm arching them." Douglas repeatedly failed to observe social convention with the other justices and staff. Although he was unable to perform his job, he refused to resign. Even after he was forced to do so, he often behaved as if he had not.

There are intriguing similarities between the reasoning and emotional deficits of individuals with damage to certain parts of their brain and the lack of empathy that characterizes people with criminal thinking patterns. They share many of the same behavioral characteristics. They don't learn from their mistakes, show little or no respect for social convention, appear to lack a moral sense, fail to anticipate consequences, and demonstrate a combination of poor decision making with a flat affect (no feeling no *empathy*).

There's another group of people short on empathy and remorse, and long on manipulation. I know you were thinking either *lawyers* or *politicians*, but I was going to mention that only one in a one hundred people in the general population are labeled "psychopaths." New research has found twenty out of one hundred *corporate executives* are psychopaths. The reference to the idea of a "successful psychopath" emerged after the 2008 financial crisis, with some people theorizing that the number of psychopaths working in the financial industry may have contributed in part to the economic crisis.

We know that too much thinking distorts reality and leaves us susceptible to anxiety and depression. On the other hand, an overreliance on our feelings can leave us vulnerable to poor impulse control and addictions. Our emotions are not generated by the brain but by the cells themselves. We need a model of mental health that acknowledges there is no separation between mind and body. There is wisdom and intelligence in the body, not just in the brain.

Your brain's job is to make up stories about how you're feeling.

Exposing our largely *unconscious* beliefs gives us the opportunity to change the way we think and take control of our lives. Accepting and acknowledging our emotions is critical because our emotions reveal the underlying beliefs we're using to cope with our experiences. It also increases our emotional intelligence by increasing our awareness of the feelings in other people.

We need a humanistic model of health that incorporates *both* our thinking and our feelings. Descartes was wrong; our ability to reason requires that we consider our feelings when making our best decisions. It's not, "I think, therefore I am," but "I feel, therefore, I'm real."

The poet e. e. cummings offers us his insight on feelings

A POET'S ADVICE

A poet is somebody who feels, and who
expresses his feelings through words.

This may sound easy. It isn't.

A lot of people think or believe or know they
feel but that's thinking or believing or
knowing: not feeling.

Almost anybody can learn to think or believe
or know, but not a single human being can be
taught how to feel. Why? Because whenever you think
or you believe or you know, you're a lot of other
people: but the moment you feel you're nobody-
but-yourself.

To be nobody-but-yourself in a world which is doing its
best, night and day, to make you everybody else means to
fight the hardest battle which any one can fight; and
never stop fighting.

As for expressing nobody-but-yourself in words, that means
working just a little harder than anybody who isn't a poet
can possibly imagine. Why? Because nothing is quite as
easy as using words like somebody else. We all do exactly
this nearly all of the time and whenever we do it, we
are not poets.

If at the end of your first ten or fifteen years of fighting
and working and feeling, you find you've written one line
of one poem, you'll be very lucky indeed.

And so my advice to all young people who wish to become
poets is: do something easy, like learning how to blow up
the world unless you're not only willing, but glad, to
feel and work and fight till you die.

Does this sound dismal? It isn't.

It's the most wonderful life on earth.

Or so I feel.

e.e. cummings

CHAPTER 9

Life Problems

Life can be tough. Everyone has problems. Here's a *short* list of my life problems: money and making a living, self-acceptance, people who are dishonest, things that make me mad, things that make me sad, other people's kids, politicians, nosey people, bad drivers, telemarketers, and barking dogs. When I got to trying to decide what to have for dinner, I was pacing back and forth, and it felt like I was just getting warmed up.

There is so much happening at such a rapid pace today that it's hard to keep things in perspective. We can lose track of the subtle nuances in life and find it difficult to distinguish what is real from what isn't real. This struggle is unavoidable. It's important to remember that everyone is unique, and everyone's reactions to their life problems will also be unique. There is no one "normal," or "right," way to live your life.

Our environment is critical to our mental health. I decided to see if I could develop a list of problems that anyone living in this constantly changing, technology- driven, toxic world must cope with day-to-day. A world where suicide is now the number one cause of death, *internationally.*

To make it onto my list, the problem had to be unavoidable, inherently stressful, a piece of the fabric of life in today's world, and so enigmatic no one seems to view it as a serious threat to our mental health. In my estimation, this list represents the cause of about 90 percent of the psychological and emotional pain we experience in this *Misinformation Age.*

Problem # 1: Oversocialization

Socialization is the process of shaping someone's behavior by establishing which behaviors society finds acceptable, or normal. A certain amount of socialization is necessary. We need a set of rules and a list of reasons to follow those rules, so we can stop waging war with each other. In addition, we need ways to enforce those rules, because some people don't want to play by the rules, and that's been a problem since Adam and Eve.

A person is considered to be well socialized if he or she accepts and adheres to the rules and moral codes of the culture they live in. It would be fair to say, however, that there is a continuum of socialization. Some people are undersocialized, some people are *well*-socialized, and some people are oversocialized.

For most of us, the socialization "agent" with the greatest influence is our own family. This is where we develop our initial set of beliefs and values and where we learn about cultural traditions, like what foods to eat, what language to speak, and how to behave "in public." This includes rules related to our gender roles and rules like what toys we're allowed to play with, *whom* we're allowed to play with, and even the games we play.

School is where we learn how to behave as a member of a group and the rules we're expected to follow to become "good citizens." We're taught rules like, "Sit up straight," "Raise your hand," and "Get in line." We hear constant reminders: "Stop talking," "Pay attention," and "Did you bring enough gum for everybody?" School is where I learned that the answer to the question "Why?," is always, "Why? Because I said so, that's why. Now, get back in line."

Because teenagers spend more time with their friends than they do with their families, peer groups have stronger correlations with personality development than parents. Twins, whose genetic makeup is identical, differ in character because they have different groups of friends, not because their parents raised them differently. Religion functions as a secondary agent of socialization, but it plays a significant role in establishing our beliefs, values, and guidelines on how to live.

Our strong tradition of human rights stands in the way of overt governmental force, so the *mass media* functions covertly as agent of socialization. The mass media has a huge influence on how things work in the world. The primary role of the mass media is to sell ideas to the public rather than inform the public. Reputations are made and broken, and fortunes are created and multiplied through the media. We need to remember Lord Acton: "Power corrupts; absolute power corrupts absolutely."

The effects of the socialization process can generate enough pressure to conform that some people can become oversocialized. These individuals spend their whole lives obeying all the rules, echoing the party line, and traveling only on the beaten path. They focus on making a good impression and worry a lot about their reputations. They believe it's okay to tell a lie if it will protect someone from getting their feelings hurt. They confuse caring with codependency. You hear them say things like, "I can't stop trying to get involved and fix the problem. It's easy for me because I like to help." Unchecked, this guilt-driven behavior and a lack of individuality can lead to a little-reported phenomenon known as "SPS" ("slow painful suicide").

I would argue that anyone who commits crimes and violence against others should be considered undersocialized. There is a long-established awareness of this problem. Billions of dollars are spent trying to identify and confine these individuals away from the *well*-socialized people who don't commit crimes.

Most oversocialized people, however, have no clue they are oversocialized. Here are some signs *you* might be oversocialized. If you've never been late on any scheduled payment, and you've never cheated on your income taxes, you might be oversocialized. If you've never cussed, "flipped off" someone in a fit of anger, or talked shit about someone *behind* his or her back, you could be oversocialized. If you've never told a lie, stolen a towel from a motel, or a taken a magazine from someone's lobby, you're almost certainly oversocialized. If you're a woman and you've never lied about your age, then you're either oversocialized, or lying. And if you routinely report all suspicious or unusual activity to the authorities, you're an oversocialized, *self*-righteous ass whom no one can stand being around.

Here are some more signs of being oversocialized:

- Codependency
- Lack of identity
- Poor interpersonal boundaries
- Dishonesty

- Martyrdom
- Secretiveness
- Enmeshment

One of the most effective ways to socialize a person is to convince him or her to freely adopt a set of preconceived notions about how he or she are supposed to live and then apply tremendous social pressure to see him or her conform. In our struggle to resist becoming oversocialized and *self*-alienated, "social pressure" is the enemy. When the social pressure to conform gets too oppressive and controlling, some people feel the need to break some rules just to maintain their sense of individuality. Some people like to drive too fast; others like to drink too much and then drive too fast; and some people use eating as a way to quell the urge to rebel against authority and the rules.

When I need to draw a line in the sand, I leave the toilet seat up, *on purpose!* If no one is looking, I'll even drink right out of the milk carton. I stop flossing and, I stop coming to a complete stop at stop signs. I know the law says I'm supposed to, but sometimes I can't control myself. I start driving around just looking for a chance to show some stop sign "who's boss." Here's what Katherine Hepburn had to say about obeying all the rules: "If you obey all the rules, you miss all the fun."

George Orwell worked for the BBC during World War II. He watched how they altered the news in the interest of control. In his book *1984*, the phrase "Big Brother" is used to refer to any overly controlling authority figure, including the government, who monitors and pressures us to conform to the rules. In the book, two institutions disseminate falsehoods for the state: *Minitrue* (a relic of the BBC) and *The Times*, a representation of "the paper of record."

The hero of Orwell's book is Winston Smith, a Nowhere Man who struggles with trying to be human in an inhuman world. Smith works in the newspapers' press room, altering history under instructions from the Party. The Party has many mottos, including: "Who controls the past controls the future: who controls the present controls the past" and "Ignorance is strength." The book inspired the adjective "Orwellian," which describes the deception, secret surveillance, and manipulation of recorded history by totalitarian or authoritarian states.

Orwell's ominous message about "fake news" and "alternative facts" is an everyday occurrence today, and no one seems to know what to do about it. Very soon we're going to be using electronic skin tattoos that rely on highly flexible electrical circuits that can bend and stretch without affecting performance. This technology will allow us to connect wirelessly to the Internet and even allow doctors to monitor our vital signs from their offices. However, there's a huge potential for abuse. Once this type of technology becomes widespread, you can say goodbye to your privacy. We'll be tracked and monitored like never before.

Talking to yourself used to be a very private affair, but that might not be the case much longer. Researchers have recorded the brain activity of people who already have electrodes implanted in their brains to treat epilepsy, while they listen to verbal speech. That brain activity can now be decoded to reveal the "silent words" we hear inside our heads.

Some researchers claim to have discovered a way to identify human emotions based on brain activity alone. They claim their research is 90 percent accurate. The question is, accurate at what? Being able to read someone's "brain activity" is not the same thing as being able to "read someone's mind." That's like putting a stethoscope on the outside wall of an airplane hangar and using what you hear to determine what's going on inside.

Problem # 2: Work

He who gives out the bread lays down the law.
SPANISH PROVERB

The Industrial Revolution gave rise to the belief that each person could someday be king. Mass education was going to destroy the class structure, and science was going to create a life of leisure through technology. Before long we started to think that we were entitled to live a life of leisure, free from the daily grind of existence. Most of us realize this kind of thinking is an empty promise. We're never going to be king, but we still get caught up in chasing the dream. We cling to the idea that if all else fails, we have our credit cards.

In the real world, big business runs the show and corporations, and financial interests establish social policy. The science funded by these groups gives them the technology to carry out their policies. Our role as individuals is to contribute to the economy as an increasingly more efficient unit of production and consumption.

We hear reports that the "unemployment rate" is about 5 percent. But when you do the research, you find that only 59 percent of Americans have jobs. That means 40 percent of Americans aren't working and don't have jobs, not 5 percent. The explanation for this discrepancy is the unemployment rate only counts people who don't have a job, but are *actively* looking for one.

The "labor force participation rate," on the other hand, includes people who can't work, have given up looking for work, or just don't want to work. The *labor force participation rate* hasn't been this low since 1977 when it was still common for women to be stay-at-home mothers. For the younger generation, not working has been attributed to the need to stay in school longer. Globalization and our rapidly expanding technology have created an economy that requires more and more education to be successful. That helps explain why the younger generation isn't working, but what explanation is there for the 40 percent of the population who aren't working and don't want to work?

Financial responsibilities can force any one of us to take a job we would prefer to walk away from. Economist E. F. Schumacher pulls no punches in giving us his perspective on why so many of us find it difficult to make peace with work:

That soul destroying, meaningless, mechanical, moronic work is an insult to human nature which must necessarily and inevitably produce either escapism or aggression, and that no amount of 'bread and circuses' can compensate for the damage done... these are the facts which are neither denied nor acknowledged but are met with an unbreakable conspiracy of silence... because to deny them would be too obviously absurd and to acknowledge them would condemn the central preoccupation of modern society as a crime against humanity.

So, work that is meaningless, mechanical, and moronic not only destroys your soul, but it's a crime against humanity. Somebody, get this man a drink!

The unfortunate truth is, all jobs have their drawbacks. It might be a daily, mind-numbing, bumper to bumper commute, back and forth to work; too much backstabbing and office politics; or spending way more time on work-related activities than we want to.

Whenever I found myself working at one crappy job or another, I would remind myself that Albert Einstein had to sell life insurance door-to-door, and work as a clerk in the U. S. Patent Office while he developed his *General Theory of Relativity*.

Most of us would reject the idea of a six-day workweek. However, in America today people are working more hours per year than at any time in recent history. A new Gallup study found full-time American workers today spend about forty-seven hours a week on their jobs. This added time comes in the form of meetings, eating lunch at our desks, or staying late to meet deadlines or to complete unfinished work. Longer hours, increased responsibilities, and the pressure to be available at all hours have become the norm for millions of working class people.

Growing expectations and smart phones can keep us tied to our work long after we've left the office. Almost 40 percent of us regularly send, receive, and check e-mails outside of working hours. During work time, the average worker checks his or her e-mail a staggering seventy-four times a day! If we enjoyed the same standard of living we had in 1948, we would work every other year or take six months off each year.

The state of Wisconsin just made it legal to work seven days a week. Employers can now request staff to work a full week, and employees can either opt in or out. I'm opting out. Some people want the extra money and opportunity to work more hours. However, this ignores the consensus that working longer hours can make you sick and less productive. This new law will likely affect blue-collar and hourly workers the most, but it will benefit some employers. Instead of hiring more people, companies can now add more hours to the schedules of existing employees.

The U. S. Travel Association has been publishing research on Americans' work and vacation habits since 1976. They report we suffer from a "work martyr complex," which leaves us chained to our work. You haven't had a vacation in a year? Neither has 135 million other Americans. More than half of American workers haven't taken a vacation in twelve months or more. We tend to measure success with things like salary, individual recognition, benefits, status, and long-term security. But when it comes to work, only your heart can tell you if you're happy.

We've already noted the escapism that economist Schumacher referred to in his indictment of meaningless work. More examples of our effort to escape can be found in our compulsive consumption and our constant need to be entertained. Not surprisingly, our favorite form of entertainment is online shopping!

For most of us, work is drudgery, that thing we do to pay the bills. I think much of our emptiness, alienation, and despair comes from this attitude toward work.

Problem # 3: Sex

> *An intellectual is a person who's found one thing*
> *more interesting than sex.*
> ALDOUS HUXLEY

The top searched marriage complaint on Google is "sexless marriage." Complaints about "sexless marriages" are *three and half times* more common than "unhappy marriage," and *eight times* more common than "loveless marriage." It turns out that sex is a lot like air; there's no problem unless you're not getting any. To many people sex is the original sin, but sex is *ubiquitous*, it's everywhere. Everyone you know has had sex, is guilty of wanting to have sex (maybe even just had sex), or is daydreaming about having sex. The birds do it, the bees do it, even flies do it.

Did you know if two flies were left to reproduce with no interruptions for a year, they would produce a mass of flies the size of the earth? Now, I'm not entirely certain what it means for two flies to reproduce "with no interruptions for a year." I'm relieved to know, however, that someone is out there on the lookout for those two flies in heat. I'm wondering though, just how fast do you need to be to interrupt two flies while they're doing it? Even though I appreciate the effort, I think this is one of those moronic, soul destroying jobs economist Schumacher was talking about.

Sex has been the subject of more lies and ruined more lives than any other human endeavor. One of the biggest lies points to the fallacy of using self-report as a means of doing research. Studies where a medical professional measured men's anatomy found the average length of the penis is somewhere in the range between 5.08 and 5.71 inches. Studies of penis length based on *self*-report however, suggest the average penis length is in the range between 6.14 and 6.54 inches!

In the 1950s, researchers experimented with the pleasurable effects of electrical stimulation of the brain on animal behavior. One famous study allowed rats to press a lever that stimulated the pleasure center of their brain. The researchers found the rats pressed the lever continuously, *several thousand* times per hour, even to the point of collapsing from fatigue. A similar study found female rats would even abandon their own newly born pups for the sake of the brain stimulation.

As a psychologist with more than a decade of experience teaching courses in *human sexuality* and *marriage and family*, you might think I would have a thing or two to say about what's normal when it comes to sex. The truth is psychology can't offer much advice when it comes to sex. Not much, except this: you need to think twice about trying to use sex to find love.

That's because men and women are fundamentally different when it comes to their views about sex. While men are daydreaming about sex, women are daydreaming about food. Also, men tend to view women as manipulative because they think women use sex as a tool for measuring their self-esteem as they do. And women tend to view men as cold and brutish because they think men have the same need for emotional connection they do.

I understand why men want to have sex because I'm a man, and we're like those rats, only worse. I've never really understood, however, why women want to have sex. I discovered some recent research that revealed 237 different reasons for why women want to have sex. Their reasons ranged from "to get rid of a headache," and "to get closer to God," and from "to become emotionally connected with my partner" to "break up a rival's relationship." Within a month of that publication, I found more research that included another forty-four reasons. This list includes my *two* favorites: "because life is short, and we could die at any moment," and "to get my boyfriend to shut up." That brings my current total to 281, but I think we've just scratched the surface.

CHAPTER 10

The Ultimate Skill

I n 1938 Harvard began studying two groups of men. Some of them were from inner-city Boston, and the others, including John F. Kennedy, studied at Harvard. The study conducted questionnaires every *two* years, interviews at different intervals, and collected health information every *five* years. The study focused on things like personalities, drinking habits, and even skull shape and size. They thought these were the things that make a difference in who you are, what your personality is like, and how happy you are.

It turned out none of these things made much of a difference. What did make a difference were the men's relationships with others. A study of adult development, transformed into a seventy-five-year study of what keeps men happy and healthy.

The fourth director of the study, Dr. Robert Waldinger, reported that the study found that good, close relationships predicted not only that these men would stay happier, but they would stay physically healthier as well. The health benefits of affectionate relationships with family, friends, and community were found to be as important as avoiding cigarettes or excessive alcohol. Dr. Waldinger, who is a Zen Buddhist priest, believes the most valuable thing we have to offer others and the key to our mental health is learning how to give someone your "full, undivided attention."

Healthy relationships are difficult to establish and hard to maintain. No matter who you are, you're going have to learn how to deal with situations involving conflicts with other people, including people you care about.

Virtually all conflicts begin with an *objective* event or experience. Our perception of the event is molded by our environment and previous experience; then it is distorted by fear because we're all secretly insecure about how to resolve a conflict.

We use various strategies to deal with our interpersonal problems. The most frequent strategy is… no strategy. We try to ignore and avoid the problem by changing the topic, minimizing it, joking around about it, or denying that a problem exists. Most of the time it requires taking a "wait and see" attitude and the hope that time will somehow resolve the conflict. Other strategies include; never giving up or always caving in, arguing, compromise, and withdrawing completely. None of these strategies, however, will resolve the conflict.

There is a skill that can help you resolve any conflict, create healthy relationships, overcome self-deception and help you become the person you were meant to be. That skill is *dialogue.* Dialogue is both a skill and a gift because it requires that you to drop any pretense, get real and accept the other person for who he or she is, and for who he or she is not, as a human being. Dialogue takes courage because it allows feelings to be honored and respected and because of what we might learn about others, and ourselves.

Socrates used dialogue as his primary teaching tool. Dialogue is most often associated with the philosopher (and one-time cave dweller) Martin Buber and his famous work, *I and Thou.* For Buber, there were only two perspectives people can take in their relationships with each other, *I-It* and *I-Thou.* When we assume an *I-It* position, we *objectify* the other person and treat him or her as a means to an end. In contrast, *I-Thou* is being authentic. Sidney Jourard, who wrote *The Transparent Self* in 1964, describes an *I-Thou* relationship as:

> *Authentic being means being oneself, honestly, in one's relations with his fellows. It means taking the first step at dropping pretenses, defenses, and duplicity. It means an end to "playing it cool," an end to using one's behavior as a gambit designed to disarm the other fellow, to get him to reveal himself before you disclose yourself to him.*

To dialogue you must learn how to genuinely express yourself and then allow that same privilege to the other person. Dialogue is a journey of self-discovery because many of our thoughts and beliefs have been unconsciously programmed into our thinking by outside influences. Don't be confused about this. Dialogue is not about finding someone to talk to.

Dialogue is about finding the courage you need to be yourself.

How to Dialogue

Dialogue requires honesty and an understanding that your point of view doesn't represent reality. Your view is simply one perspective out of many. Dialogue is more than simply finding common ground. Dialogue requires that you know the difference between self-disclosure and self-presentation.

There is a precise method and the process requires four things:

1) The right "attitude,"
2) Knowing the difference between *sympathy* and *empathy*,
3) Knowing the difference between *listening* and *hearing*, and
4) Emotional Intelligence (EQ).

(1) The Right "Attitude"

Amy Cuddy, a psychologist at the Harvard Business School, has been studying first impressions for more than a decade. She and her colleagues have found we decide whether or not we like someone within the first seven seconds of meeting them. To make that decision, we ask ourselves two primary questions: "Can I trust this person?" and "Can I respect this person's capabilities?" Once we answer those two questions, we spend the rest of our time finding ways to justify our decision.

This seven-second judgment is the antithesis of *dialogue*. The goal in dialogue is to cultivate what Zen masters refer to as a "beginner's mind," where you learn to perceive with as little preconception as possible. There is a well-traveled story about a man who approached a Japanese master to learn about Zen. The master served him some tea. When the man's cup was full, the master kept pouring, and the tea spilled out of the cup and onto the table.

"The cup is full!" cried the man. "It won't hold any more tea."

"Like this cup," said the master, "you are full of your own opinions and assumptions. How can I show you Zen unless you first empty your cup?"

The utility of the empty cup is its emptiness.

(2) The Difference between *Sympathy* and *Empathy*

When we look around and find ourselves enmeshed in the same struggles as everyone else, we start to think we understand how other people are feeling. *Sympathy* can be a sign of being more involved in someone else's life than your own. That's because *sympathy* is thinking about a feeling; it's not a feeling.

Empathy, on the other hand, is identifying with what another person is feeling and matching that same feeling. Empathy requires you to refrain from imposing your thoughts and feelings onto the other person. Empathy is what you feel when you look into someone else's eyes.

To teach men the difference between *sympathy* and *empathy*, researchers have developed a way to mimic labor pains through electrical stimulation. Electrodes are strategically placed on the man's body to simulate the pain associated with child birth. Following their ordeal with those electrodes, the men who participated in the project reported a deeper and more profound connection with their wives. They now understand at a feeling level (empathy) what their wives go through while giving birth.

(3) Listening versus Hearing

Contrary to what you might think, the most important part of learning how to dialogue is being able to listen when someone else speaks. Hearing is a word we use to describe the *physiological* process by which sounds are received by our ears and then transmitted to the brain. Listening, on the other hand, refers to the *psychological* process of interpreting and understanding what we hear. Dialogue requires you to learn how to give the individual before you your "full, undivided attention."

Our nonverbal behavior was the only language we used to communicate throughout most of human history. As a consequence, by the time we're six months old, virtually every human being has inherited the ability to recognize certain emotions in other people's facial expressions. Unfortunately, social pressure causes us to ignore these important cues in our interpersonal communications.

(4) Emotional Intelligence (EQ)

Learning how to dialogue requires that you learn to ignore the temptation to nod your head every so often to convince the other person you were listening when you weren't. The essence of dialogue is great listening skills, and it involves responding *reflectively* to what you heard the other person say. That means restating, in your own words, both the content and the underlying emotional message in what you heard.

Dialogue requires mastering two different skills, "active listening" and "paraphrasing." *Active listening* is focusing on the subtle cues like body language, tone of voice, and inflection that accompany the words people use when they speak. Once you listen to what someone says, the next step is to *paraphrase* what you heard, back to him or her.

To succeed, you have to try to see through the other person's eyes, sense what he or she is feeling, and then put that understanding into words the other person can recognize. Your goal is to articulate, if you can, that person's intended message, so he or she feels understood. You can reawaken your instinctive ability to connect with other people's feelings if you learn to refrain from passing judgment. Simply listen; if you mishear the person, or misunderstand what he or she meant to say, he or she will be happy to correct you. The person will realize you were paying attention, or at least trying to. **Learning these two skills will improve your life and your relationships, today.**

Dialogue Is Intimacy

The psychiatrist R. D. Laing became internationally famous for his radical experiment with alternative ways of treating schizophrenia. Laing established Kingsley Hall, which was a residential household for people looking for an alternative to being hospitalized. There was no paid staff, and no one had an assigned role. Since no "treatment" was provided for the residents, the question becomes: what is the healing or therapeutic agent if there was no overt treatment? The answer is that Kingsley Hall represented Laing's observation that the person with schizophrenia has no friends and needs opportunities to make friends with people he or she would otherwise avoid.

The individuals at Kingsley Hall lived together without any structured treatment, and they were free to form genuine relationships with each other. This process was allowed to occur spontaneously, with no attempts made at matchmaking. Laing referred to it as a "melting pot where preconceptions were melted down in the nitty-gritty of living together."

While the people at Kingsley Hall were free to make friends, they were also free *not* to make friends. Most of the residents there were in open revolt against conventional society. In particular, they found it difficult to establish a "public self" the average person accepts as a matter of necessity. This *public self* is the social facade we use in our nonintimate dealings with other people.

It was Alfred Adler's observation that schizophrenia isn't a break with reality, but a break with *sincerity*. People typically labeled with "schizophrenia" know that what they are saying and reporting may be bizarre or outside the norm, but they don't care. They just don't want to play the conformity game any longer.

Laing also observed that these individuals had trouble enjoying their own company and lacked the motivation to pursue their own interests. Given the families they came from, their time at Kingsley Hall may have been the first time they had ever been exposed to people being kind to each other or treating each other with love and affection.

Sigmund Freud believed a therapeutic relationship is one where the therapist never passes judgment on the patient. Freud referred to this trait as "neutrality." He believed this lack of judgment is so rare that when we encounter it, it elicits a potentially transformative experience. Toward the end of his life Freud concluded that talking to each other in this special way (dialogue) is so powerful, he labeled it the "talking cure." That's high praise from "the Man" himself.

The Original Conflict

The most important part of communication isn't in the words, but in the meanings. Conflict always involves some ambiguity about what something means. The same communication can have different meanings for different people. Consider, for example, as we look at what might be the original interpersonal conflict: the story of Adam and Eve.

The story revolves around Eve, who is unable to resist her attraction to the symbol of Adam's sexuality (I know what you're thinking, but it turns out it's the snake). Driven by lust, she tastes the forbidden fruit of desire, with which she then tempts Adam, who also succumbs. In the end, God banishes them both from the Garden of Eden.

There are several different *meanings* people attribute to the story. Some people see a great deal of sexual imagery; from the snake to the forbidden fruit, to temptation, to a possible incestuous brother/sister, husband/wife relationship between Adam and Eve.

Other people find the story symbolic of intellectual awakening, self-discovery and knowledge. And some people view the expulsion of Adam and Eve from the garden of Eden as symbolic of the rise of rules and, with them, rule-breaking and punishment.

In *Genesis*, God asks:

God to Adam: Is it true Adam that you ate the fruit of the tree I warned you not to eat?

Adam to God: That woman you gave me, it was her fault. She tempted me.

God to Eve: Is it true, Eve, that you tempted Adam to eat the fruit?

Eve to God: It was his fault. He started waving that thing around. What was I supposed to do?

Adam to Eve: My fault! It was your fault. You and that damned snake.

Eve to Adam: There you go again, trying to blame someone else for your mistake. You chose to take that bite. I didn't force you to do anything. Besides, you never warned me about the snake.

Adam to Eve: You're so coy, prancing around in that little fig leaf, pretending like you didn't know what was going on.

Eve to Adam: You just don't want to take responsibility for your mistakes.

Adam to Eve: My biggest mistake was listening to you.

Eve to Adam: You can go to hell.

What if... instead of Adam and Eve getting enmeshed in a conflict/drama, they had remembered to **RELAX** and ask themselves the **Five (5) Critical Questions**?

What is the issue?

If the issue is what we can see from a video recording of the conflict (the facts), then the issue is Adam and Eve ate the fruit that God warned them not to eat.

What are you feeling?

What are they feeling?

Whose drama is this?

Adam concluded that God was angry, Eve was hurt and angry, and Adam was ashamed. The drama appears to be that Adam and Eve disobeyed God and ate the fruit they weren't supposed to eat. However, God created this drama, since he created the apple, the snake, and the potential for conflict. He's trying to draw both Adam and Eve into this drama by trying to establish what it *means* that they ignored his warning and ate the fruit.

What if... We change the meaning?

Adam asks himself: Why would an omniscient, all-seeing and all-knowing Creator create the "Apple Drama" and then pretend that he didn't know that we took a bite of the apple? And, why would he endow us with curiosity, unless he wanted us to use it? And finally, he didn't warn either of us about the snake, or the desire he placed in us to taste the forbidden fruit.

Adam concluded that God created this conflict as a test. However, he determined their sin wasn't eating the apple. Their sin was trying to place the blame for their behavior on someone other than themselves. From this perspective, it wasn't God, but Adam and Eve who expelled themselves from the garden but not for eating the apple. They were expelled for not taking responsibility for what they did. Changing the meaning allowed Adam to gain a new perspective and use the insight(s) he learned to get real. That choice changed the outcome of the story.

God to Adam: Is it true Adam that you ate the fruit from the tree, I warned you not to eat?

Adam to God: Yes God, and it was... *d e l i c i o u s!*

Adam to Eve: Eve, I apologize to you for trying to shift the blame onto you. You're right; no one forced me to take that bite; it was my choice. He didn't warn either of us about the snake, either. He put it here to see what we would do. In the future, I think we should *dialogue* things like this. We can share our thoughts, honor our feelings, be responsible, and avoid the wrath of you-know-who.

"You want another bite of the apple?"

CHAPTER 11

Are You Growing Up or Just Growing Older?

Have you ever noticed how adults are always asking kids what they want to be when they grow up? That's because they're looking for ideas. A critical part of growing up is discovering who you are and what you want.

One of the great discourses on the stages of development we go through in life is Shakespeare's monologue in *As You Like It*. It begins, "All the world's a stage, and all the men and women merely players." The speech compares the world to a stage and life to a play and catalogs what Shakespeare believed were the *seven* stages of a man's life. The German psychologist Erik Erikson wrote about *eight* stages of *psychosocial development*, and Jean Piaget, the Swiss psychologist wrote about *four* key stages of *cognitive development*. The "Hero's Journey" is a metaphor for the stages of development we go through toward enlightenment: moving on from dependence to conformity, to self-discovery, and then onto learning how to develop healthy relationships with other people.

Much of what we consider to be healthy or unhealthy, normal or abnormal, depends on the culture and time we live. The culture and our environment change, even if we don't. Over 86 percent of American adults today use the Internet, and 76 percent of them check their Facebook account daily.

I wondered if there might be a correlation between intelligence and mental health. Maybe "smart" people are more likely to learn and adapt to change better than the rest of us. I found no evidence to suggest that those people we might consider to be "smart," are happier, or better-adjusted to life's struggles than the rest of us.

Isaac Newton was a head case. He was petty, vindictive, and a total jerk. He had manic episodes where he would work for days without eating or sleeping. After that he would fall into a deep depression, experience auditory and visual hallucinations, and refuse to speak to anyone. Today, we label that, "bipolar disorder."

Albert Einstein would very likely be diagnosed as suffering from Asperger's syndrome. This is a condition now considered a part of autism that is characterized by higher-than-average intelligence coupled with impaired social skills. It often involves repetitive patterns of interests and activities things like advanced mathematics and *physics*.

It was reported that Albert actually made his wife sign a contract that stipulated there would be "no intimacy." The contract stipulated that she was to serve him three meals a day "in his room" and detailed precisely what she was to do with his laundry.

Frank Lloyd Wright was a total non-conformist and was well known for his *narcissism* and colossal ego: "Early in life I had to choose between honest arrogance and hypocritical humility, I chose the former."

Howard Hughes and Nicola Tesla both had intense phobias of dirt and germs and Tesla did everything in multiples of three. He lived in hotels for years without ever paying his bills. George Gershwin was restless, unruly and hyperactive like a kid diagnosed with ADHD. I also discovered that authors are more likely to be depressed than the general population. The Roman philosopher Seneca wrote, "There is no great genius without a tincture of madness."

Isaac Newton, Albert Einstein, Nicola Tesla, and Frank Lloyd Wright all had the *courage* they needed to be themselves. It's also certain they each had a calling, a challenge, or a dream that they were committed to. What they all lacked were the interpersonal skills they needed to develop healthy relationships with other people.

Growth Requires Change

It's been my experience that most people change *only* when they are convinced the pain of staying the same far outweighs the pain of changing. However, the pain we try so hard to avoid leaves us without one of the great motivations to change: pain. Instead of embracing the need to change and grow, we try to ignore or avoid our feelings. If that doesn't work, there's alcohol, as well as legal and illegal drugs.

Our failure to grow and change leaves us stuck in one developmental stage or another. As a consequence, we lose touch with our "self" and end up feeling sad, lonely, and depressed. These are not symptoms of "mental illness"; these are universal and predictable human responses associated with our struggle to deal with change. If we get a little too comfortable with dodging, avoiding and denying our feelings, our *apathy* can reach *critical mass*, and when this happens we lose touch with our hopes and dreams as well. Now we're no longer talking about depression; now we're describing "depersonalization."

Depersonalization is the result of ignoring our own interests and becoming strangers to ourselves. A culture that values conformity, dependence, and predictability over authenticity creates Nowhere Men, and Mr. Duffys. These are people who have gotten lost in the struggle just to survive. They no longer have a point of view, only see what they want to see, and have forgotten about their hopes and dreams. They feel numb and empty because they have lost contact with the critical part of what makes them special and unique. I believe the worldwide epidemic and global disease burden WHO is talking about isn't depression, but rather depersonalization.

I believe that what we label and accept as "normal" in this culture today are people functioning somewhere between 35 and 55 percent of their true capacity. That's all that remains of their *human spirit* after sacrificing and censoring themselves to fit it and be accepted. That means they never get the opportunity to feel great passion, know great joy, or reach their true potential. I'm not suggesting here that the mentally healthy person is perfect and functions at 100 percent. The truly healthy person is someone who has lied, suffered the effects of lying, learned and grown from the experience, and then struggled to recover his or her authenticity.

Recovery from a culture that has normalized dishonesty requires a *conscious* commitment to avoid becoming dishonest ourselves. Whether its fake news, alternate facts, omitting important information, being ambiguous, saying nothing, letting the other person believe an untruth, fraud, exaggeration, hypocrisy, or straight- up lying, we have come to accept dishonesty as a part of life.

Being dishonest turns our lives into tangled webs of deception, half-truths, and manipulation. Our tacit acceptance of this behavior is preventing us from developing the authentic relationships we need to be truly healthy. It's silently and in gentle, barely noticeable ways, stealing our lives away from us. Being dishonest destroys our integrity, arrests our growth, compromises our immune systems, and negatively affects our *psychological* and *physical* well-being. Being dishonest is more damaging to our health than smoking.

Recovering Our Authenticity

We need three things to maintain our *human spirit* and be mentally healthy. We need the *courage* to be ourselves, to be genuine, to be real. We also need a challenge, a commitment to something bigger and more important than simply our survival. We need something to survive for. Finally, we need to be able to establish and maintain an emotional connection with other people. That means demonstrating honesty, empathy, and intimacy.

Here's the problem, being honest and real has been espoused for millennia, but most people don't believe in it for a second. They think it's naive and even foolish to try to live and behave *authentically*. They justify their dishonesty with euphemisms like tact and diplomacy, sensitivity to the feelings of others, and discretion. This reinforces the belief that we're too weak to handle the truth. George Orwell described the kind of courage it takes to get real and be honest when he wrote, "During times of universal deceit, telling the truth becomes a revolutionary act."

Research has shown that we are more likely to experience a "mental illness" than we are to develop diabetes, heart disease, or any type of cancer combined. Here's the good news: most people eventually outgrow their emotional problems even without any intervention. The newest research also suggests that most common psychological problems are short-lived. Lots and lots of people diagnosed with a "mental illness" get better, mostly when their social lives improve.

However, if you think that truth is going to turn this medication-driven, train-wreck, mental health-care system around, you're as naïve as I was. You can thank *Big Pharma* and job security for that. There are thousands and thousands of jobs at stake and millions and millions of dollars to make. Those pharmaceutical companies aren't going to sit idly by and let all that money slip away. We're still going to hear the next great miracle cure is some new drug.

The Power of Thoughts

One of the great insights emerging from neuroscience is the knowledge that the adult human brain retains much of the plasticity of the developing brain of a baby. We now know that changes in the brain can be generated by pure mental activity alone. Something as *subjective* as a thought can act back on the physical stuff of the brain. Our willful effort, or *intentionality* (human spirit), changes how the brain works and even its physical structure. Your mind can change your brain.

The popularity of "multitasking" as a way to be more productive is a widely held belief without any support. People who attempt to multitask are 40 percent *less* productive. Trying to do two cognitive things at the same time simply can't be done. We can only focus our attention on one thing at a time, however, we can shift our focus from one thing to another with astonishing speed. Despite how quickly we can shift our focus, this "task-shifting" is incredibly unproductive.

Everything we have learned about the brain and nervous system tells us that mental fitness is like physical fitness. Whether it's shooting free throws, learning how to communicate better, or learning how to control our thinking, if we practice at it, we get better at it.

The National Institute of Mental Health currently has over five hundred scientific studies documenting the benefits "mindfulness" can have on our mental health. *Mindfulness* is the awareness and acceptance of present experience. It's not emptying your mind, or ignoring uncomfortable feelings, or avoiding life's problems. It's embracing and accepting life as it is. More importantly, mindfulness is not a personality trait but a state achieved through practice.

Being mindful starts with accepting the fact we can never be completely aware of everything that's going on. Mindfulness is learning how to be more focused on what we pay attention to. You can't turn your brain off, but you can learn to observe your negative thinking and disturbing thoughts, recognize them, and not get caught up in believing them.

Even when we try to monitor our thoughts, our attention span is only about eight seconds, so it's difficult to pay attention for very long. However, each time we notice we've gotten lost in our thoughts, we can bring ourselves back. We simply get back to focusing our attention, while balancing on that tightrope of external *objective* experiences together *with* the internally generated *subjective* experiences that make up our world. The goal is to learn how to use that sense of awareness to become conscious of the decisions we make.

We leave our potential trapped inside the cave when we don't accept the challenge to be ourselves. Each time we accept and honor our feelings, without judging them or trying to ignore them, we create a new perspective from which to view a problem or conflict. However, for that insight to become transforming, we have to understand we're not passive participants in the creation of our lives.

Some people, after years of counseling and therapy, sometimes manage to gain insight into why they did what they did and how they got themselves into the mess they got themselves into. The problem is, understanding is never enough. To change and grow, we have to develop new skills by trying something new and learning from our mistakes.

Controlling Our Thinking

When we maintain a "safe" emotional distance from other people, it leaves us emotionally numb and stuck in survival mode. As a consequence, we never develop a true sense of who we are. Ken Wilber said it best, telling the truth won't necessarily set you free, but truthfulness will. The question we need to be asking ourselves is this: Am I being honest and genuine, or am I sacrificing my integrity to fit in and be accepted? Remember Socrates, "To find yourself, think for yourself."

Dealing with a system that refuses to listen to reason and turns our vulnerabilities into pathology changed my thinking from treating symptoms to teaching skills. In particular, I began teaching the people I work with a set of skills including critical thinking, advanced communication, and emotional regulation skills. These are the core skills taught to mental health professionals in graduate school. My goal was to teach active listening, paraphrasing, and rapport building skills. There is magic in this set of skills, I can assure you.

It's ironic, but the most effective therapists are those who break most of the rules taught in psychotherapy training. They are honest and genuine in the presence of their clients, and they have learned that the most useful model of psychotherapy is the experience of being permitted to be oneself. It turns out that eliciting "real self" behavior in others is accomplished best by manifesting in ourselves. You get what you sow. If you want the truth, tell the truth.

Rapport

The word *rapport* comes from the French verb *rapporter,* which means "to carry something back." Rapport is taught in graduate schools to prospective therapists as the basis of effective therapy. Without it, there is no therapeutic relationship. Rapport is a critical piece of effective communication because it demonstrates *empathy.* In terms of how people can use rapport to better relate to each other, it means what one person sends out the other sends back. Learn to establish rapport whenever you communicate with other people. This should be your priority.

There are a number of techniques that can be helpful in building rapport. Matching body language, maintaining eye contact, and matching breathing rhythms all take time to learn and can seem disingenuous if done poorly. There is an effective way to develop rapport, and you don't need a doctorate in psychology to learn and use it. The process is called "paraphrasing."

Our interpersonal communication involves both words and feelings. Simply repeating the words that someone else uses will kill effective communication. However, sensing and acknowledging another person's underlying emotion and then confirming your observation with a question will turn you into a world class communicator.

I use it all day, every day. I use it in my professional life, in my casual interactions with other people, and even with my wife, because it enhances effective communication and minimizes conflict. Here's a *paraphrase* with all the basics to get you started: you have to give the other person your "full, undivided attention" and then fill in the blanks.

"Let me see if I was listening. You're feeling [blank] because of [blank] and [blank] and you want me (or someone) to [blank] is that right?"

We don't really discover who we are until we learn to share our typically *private* thoughts and feelings with others. The secret to the therapeutic process, self-discovery, and our mental health is *self*-honesty and honesty in our communications with others. Our well-being, including our mental health, comes from being listened to and having our individuality acknowledged and respected.

CHAPTER 12

A Manifesto of Mental Health

A manifesto is a statement of principles and intentions that challenges existing beliefs, fosters commitment, and provokes change. The Declaration of Independence is a manifesto, and so is Dr. Martin Luther King's "I Have a Dream" speech. More importantly, a manifesto is a call to action. I set out on a quest to define "mental health," and thirty years later, I'm sharing what I found in a manifesto of mental health.

To be honest, I didn't really want to write this book. I thought one of those ivory tower guys, with impressive credentials and a distinguished academic position, should write the book. I thought those credentials would wake people up; they would come to their senses and things would change. So, I waited and waited, and waited and waited, because I knew the book was going to stir up some deep emotions, expose some painful truths, and be a lot of hard work. Since I am lazy by nature, I just wanted to *buy* this book. I was ready and waiting to jump onto the bandwagon.

Beliefs are difficult to change because they become so deeply ingrained. Consider that in 1976, a Nobel Prize was awarded for the discovery that the degenerative brain disease called "kuru" is caused by a slow virus that remains dormant for years before it does any harm. Two decades later, in 1997, another Nobel Prize was awarded for demonstrating that the cause of "kuru" is not a virus at all, but rather by a misshapen protein called a "prion." For more than two decades, medical science was wrong.

All of us started out our lives as little warriors, fearless, naturally curious, and full of self-confidence. We used this healthy self-reliance to teach ourselves how to walk and talk, as well as the subtle social rules of the culture we are born into. Every time we failed, we regrouped, started over, and tried again. It never occurred to us to give up and stop trying. We learned from our mistakes, and we put what we learned into action.

Then, a sophisticated social system took over and filled our heads with a bunch of preconceived ideas about how we're supposed to behave if we want to fit in and be accepted. We're taught to value our roles over our emotions, hopes, and dreams. We're taught not to be selfish, warned that only certain kinds of thoughts and feelings are acceptable, and encouraged to let our conscience be our guide. For most of us, however, our conscience consists of the beliefs and thinking the social system put there. And, being genuine and self-reliant is not being selfish.

It's hard to be healthy when your head is full of preconceived notions about life. By the time we reach adulthood most of us have lost touch with our real "self." This pre-programmed thinking must be exposed and replaced with honesty and authenticity. Someone cut the first umbilical cord for us, but we have to cut the *over*dependency cord for ourselves. That means learning how to do our own thinking and make our own decisions. Taking responsibility gives us the opportunity to learn from our mistakes, change, and grow like we did when we were little self-reliant warriors.

The Subjective Side of Life

Are *subjective* experiences like thoughts and feelings as real as basketballs? I know I spend about 90 percent of my time inside my head, consumed with my thoughts and feelings, so they're very real to me. You might say, however, that basketballs are more "real" because you can see and bounce a basketball, but you can't see or touch thoughts and feelings.

There's a large part of the world that is real, but invisible. This subjective, hidden reality presents a dilemma because it means that everyone's view of reality is just as real as the next person's, only different. The problems begin when we try to decide whose reality we are going to use when we want to communicate, mine or yours?

The *subjective* side of life is where artists find the inspiration for the art they create and where poets and philosophers find the motivation they need for the things they write. We need our thoughts and feelings as much as we need oxygen. If you go too long without oxygen, you can lose your life. If you go too long without your feelings, you can lose touch with your "self." The *subjective* side of your life, including your hopes and dreams, is the center of *your* universe.

Some people experience the *subjective* side of life like they're standing in front of one of those big glass enclosures at the Monterey Bay Aquarium. There's a lot of information to process, things are constantly changing, and it's hard to stay focused on one thing for very long.

Without any structure to put it all into context, the experience becomes mesmerizing, and you can end up in a trance. You become just a passive observer of a vast, and important part of your life. If you look closely, however, there is a structure and a *dynamic* and ongoing relationship between our mostly *unconscious* beliefs, our thinking patterns, and our emotional states.

Everyone's thoughts are their own (and thank God for that!), but feelings are universal. Everyone has feelings. For most of human history, those feelings were the primary means we used to communicate with each other. Even after the introduction of language, over 90 percent of our communication is still *non*verbal. Our feelings, not our words, are the "coins of the realm" of our relationships with other people. Without our feelings, we can't experience empathy; and without empathy, we can't develop intimacy.

The thought of exposing their secret, inner world is a terrifying thought for many people. Self-disclosure requires real courage because we have become as opaque to ourselves as we have to others. Learning to speak in the first person about your experiences, and then allowing others that same privilege, is how we discover who we are, establish empathy, and experience intimacy in our relationships. The challenge is to maintain our sense of balance on that tightrope of *objective* and *subjective* experiences we call reality. If you lose your balance, someone might think you have a mental illness or something.

A Call to Action

Our lives have become deeply superficial. We keep our conversations limited to niceties so we don't have an effective way to communicate with each other.

More important, we don't know how to express ourselves effectively. That "safe" emotional distance we keep from each other leaves us feeling disconnected from each other and apathy slowly infects our lives. I believe nothing makes a person sick, mentally and physically, faster than feeling disinterested, disconnected, and unaccepted.

I believe any success I have helping people has been due primarily to their motivation to change. We can't fix people or change people, but we can inspire people to change themselves by reconnecting them with their hopes and dreams. The best way to do that is self-discovery through self-disclosure.

How can anyone know you unless you make yourself known to them through honest self-disclosure?

How can anyone be expected to meet your needs, if you won't make them known?

And, how can you know your own needs if you have become estranged from your real self?

Warriors understand that its society's job to tame the individual and the individual's job to remain free. It's always been this way. A warrior, today, is a revolutionary who stands up the temptation to be lulled into being dishonest and *in*authentic. Heroes accept the challenge, but it takes a warrior's spirit and courage to succeed because warriors have to develop a backbone, not a wishbone.

How about you? Are ready to drop your defenses and pretenses and be a warrior, or are you content with being just another casualty?

When it comes down to it, it doesn't matter what others think about us anyway. When they criticize us, we get defensive, and when they complement us we don't believe them. We need to stop focusing on maintaining our reputation and focus on developing our integrity and character. The only praise we really crave is our own.

The INSIGHT Model of Communication creates an intellectual structure we can use to communicate effectively with each other. Since everyone's nervous system operates in precisely the same way, each person's reality can be expressed as their *objective* (facts), *subjective* (thoughts and feelings) and *inter-subjective* (meanings) experiences. Learning to speak about these three realities in the first person is the secret to self-discovery, the basis of genuine relationships, and the key to our happiness.

The **Five (5) Critical Questions** expands the "facts, feelings and meanings" model to reveal the relationship between our beliefs, our emotions, and our thinking patterns. Asking and answering the questions gives you the opportunity to integrate your *conscious* mind with your *unconscious* emotional body. The questions establish an "observing awareness" or "working memory," and that pause gives you the chance to establish and maintain your awareness of our *objective* and *subjective* experiences.

No Regrets

As people age and approach their mortality, they report they have more regrets about the things they didn't do, than any remorse they have for the mistakes they made in their lives. Here's a list of the top five regrets people express as they approach the final twelve weeks of their lives:

> **(1) I wish I'd had the courage to live a life true to myself, not the life others had expected of me.**
> **(2) I wish I hadn't worked so hard.**
> **(3) I wish I had dared to express my feelings.**
> **(4) I wish I hadn't let old friends slip away.**
> **(5) I wish I hadn't been so afraid of change.**

When you commit to being yourself and focusing on those things that are meaningful to you, you might notice some people retreat, disengage, and even take an emotional "safe" step back. They might even say things behind your back. That's because they're incapable of seeing the universe inside you. They have sight, but no vision.

The only reality is the one you create for yourself. No matter how much your family or your friends or *Big Brother* want you to live the way they think you should live, it's your life. You matter and your dreams matter, so you have to honor what feels right in your heart.

How sad would it be if you get to end of your life and you realize you never lived your life?

Living your life means, *first* and foremost, discovering your "real" self and then committing to a purpose or something meaningful to *you*, something that replenishes your *humanium* and *human spirit*. The mantra for mental health is do *The Walk of Life.* Be yourself, and do your thing.

I sincerely hope we meet one day, each of us doing *The Walk of Life.* If we do, I hope this book becomes a starting point for a dialogue about mental health. I've done my best to be transparent by sharing my personal experiences with my struggle to continuously grow and change into the person I want to be. Now that I've had my say, I'm ready to give you my full, undivided attention.

www.ingramcontent.com/pod-product-compliance
Lightning Source LLC
Chambersburg PA
CBHW070812280726
48660CB00015B/421